Choices

Choices

A Story of Survival

M. KAY RUNYAN

This book is dedicated to my children,
Daniel, April, and David

CONTENTS

1 RED RIVER VALLEY

When I was born on May 1, 1943, my Southern Baptist parents inexplicably gave me a strong Irish Catholic name, Mary Katherine Runyan. It's a name I have never used.

I've gone by variations of the name over the years—sometimes Kay, sometimes Kathy—but for the first few years of my life, I was known simply as "Kay-Doll."

My big brother Ben, who was a year old at the time of my birth, could not pronounce "Kathy," my mother's chosen moniker for me. He could only manage to say "Kay." He was so convinced I was actually a little doll that "Doll" was soon added to "Kay."

I loved my big brother, and many of my childhood memories revolved around the fun we had together—as well as the scrapes he got me into—as we roamed around the land where our father grew tomatoes in the Red River Valley of Texas in the 1940s.

One day, when I was about four years old, I sat inside a bushel basket atop a wooden sled out in the field, clutching a big toad frog. Our mule, Amos, pulled the sled across the field as I sat surrounded by tomato seedlings and watched Ben running around, aimlessly throwing clods of dirt.

I turned my attention to studying my frog intently. It was brown, with circles on its back outlined in black, and it had a whitish belly. Its long hind legs dangled from its body as it stared at me from the eyes on the side of its head. As I looked at my frog, Ben stopped throwing dirt and came over.

"Look, Ben," I said. "My shog's eyes are on the side of its head!" (I couldn't pronounce the letter "f" so it usually came out "sh.")

"Of course he has eyes on the side of his head, stupid!" Ben retorted. "Didn't you know that?" He always pretended to know more than I did. With that he walked off and resumed chunking clods of dirt at anything and everything.

I went back to studying my frog. This was *my* frog and I loved it. In fact, I thought I should kiss it, but before I had a chance, Amos the mule bolted.

Everything went flying from the sled, including me in my bushel basket. My prized frog jumped out of my hands as I landed in the dirt and screamed at the top of my lungs.

My other big brother, fourteen-year-old Gerald, grabbed the mule's reins and shouted, "Whoa, *durn it!*"

"Gerald Ray!" Daddy yelled, "Get that mule under control!"

Ben stared at the commotion, but not for long. Mother grabbed him and promptly gave him a good whipping because he was the one who had thrown the clod of dirt at poor Amos the mule, hitting him on the rear end and making him bolt.

Daddy and my big sister Barbara, who was twelve, picked up the spilled seedlings and put them back on the sled.

I sat in the dirt and cried as my frog jumped away. Gerald put the bushel basket back on the sled and deposited me into it once more. Watching my frog take great long leaps across the field, I was afraid Ben would get him, so I screamed louder.

Gerald was exasperated. "What's the matter with you, Kay-Doll? You don't look hurt!"

"I lost my shog!" I cried.

Gerald saw the frog hopping to safety and ran after it. He grabbed it and placed it my hands, assuring me, "There now, here's your shog."

I held my frog tightly and kissed him, not just once, but several times.

While all this was happening, my aunt walked to the field with a jar of iced tea. Witnessing the commotion, she bent over and laughed so hard she peed her pants. A wet pool formed on the ground below her, and when we all saw it, the whole family began laughing until our sides hurt.

"What in tarnation started all *that*?" she asked, but we were laughing much too hard to answer.

Laughter was something to be enjoyed back then, when it could be had, because making a living in East Texas was a struggle for my family.

The Red River Valley had good bottom land where most crops grew. Mostly it was poor farmers like Daddy and Mother, working in the fields every day from sunup to sundown. Daddy grew tomatoes on someone else's land. The weather could ruin or make a crop. Too much rain destroyed the fields of tomatoes, and too little dried them up. Even at four years of age I could tell how dead tired Mother and Daddy were when they staggered into our house at sundown with aching backs. Barbara and Gerald worked tirelessly as Ben and I trotted along next to them.

As soon as we returned to the house, my job was to run over and start pumping water into the dishpan so Mother and Barbara could wash up and begin working again, this time preparing supper. The heat from the wood-burning stove made the temperature inside the little house unbearable, and the sweat poured down their faces as they were cooking.

Every planting season Daddy plowed long furrows to set the tomato plants in. The seedling tomatoes were placed on the sled that had been made from planks and two-by-fours, and Amos the mule was hooked up to the sled. Gerald led Amos up and down the rows so Mother and Barbara could place the seedlings in the long furrows. Daddy then came behind and put dirt around the plants.

I didn't know any other kind of life, so I was happy.

I was born in the house on the farm. The first room one walked into from outside was the kitchen. A door led from the kitchen to the porch, where the water pump came up from a pipe in the ground. I loved to pump the handle up and down and watch water pour out of the spout. I could barely reach the handle, so I stood on an empty crate to get the leverage I needed. If we needed hot water, it had to be heated on the wood cookstove, which stood in the middle of the room. The slop bucket that we used for feeding the pigs sat on the floor by the stove. It was my and Ben's job to take the bucket, go to the pig pen, and dump the leftover scraps into the trough. We stood back and watched the little pigs shoulder each other out of the way, trying to eat as much as they could before momma hog got to it. Later in life, whenever I heard the phrase, "eating like a pig," I'd envision our pigs trying to eat all the food as fast as they could.

Mother taught me how to gather the eggs from our chickens. She warned me to always look in the nests first because a snake might be in there, eating the eggs. I felt very responsible and grown up when I handed over the eggs to Mother and she could see that there wasn't a single broken egg.

I was too young to realize that my life would soon change because Daddy wanted an escape from the back-breaking work of farming. One night I heard him talking to Mother about how much he wanted to do something different. He wrote letters to our relatives, letting them know that he wanted to stop raising tomatoes and find other work.

Not too many weeks after that, I was awakened by Mother one morning as she yanked the bed covers back and said, "Get out of the bed. Hurry up and get dressed!"

I didn't know what was happening, but I knew I wasn't going to ride on the sled that day. "Are we going somewhere?" I asked, but she had already left the room.

I could hear a commotion taking place. Mother, Daddy, Gerald, and Barbara were going in and out of the front door, carrying our belongings. I was confused and started to cry. Barbara gave me a cold biscuit and said, "Stop crying!" before she returned to helping Mother take our things to the car. When the car and small trailer were loaded, Mother told Ben and me to get in.

One of Daddy's cousins had told him about a man who owned a farm in Texarkana, Texas. This fellow needed a family to live on the farm and take care of the chickens and livestock, as well as to grow bedding plants for his feed store. Daddy said it had to be better than what we were doing now to make a living. I listened to everyone talking and wanted to ask questions but I couldn't. I was what Mother called "tongue-tied," even though thoughts were swirling around in my head like a tornado.

"How far away are we moving?" Gerald asked.

"It's about fifty miles," Daddy said. "We'll be in the car for a while."

I saw Amos the mule standing by the barn. Our dog, Spooken, was in the yard. I began crying because I thought they were going to be left behind, but no one paid any attention to my tears. Finally, when everything had been loaded into the car and trailer, Mother whistled for Spooken to get in the car. I felt a surge of relief and happiness as I pulled Spooken close to me and hugged him tightly.

"But how are we going to move Amos?" I asked my brother Gerald.

"A neighbor will bring him," he assured me. Daddy had paid a neighbor with a horse trailer to haul our mule to Texarkana. Amos would be needed to plow the field for the bedding plants.

I was sad to leave our farm as it had been the only home I'd ever known, but I was also excited to be moving to a new place.

Finally we were all in the car and ready to go. We were squished together with hardly any room to move—Barbara, Ben, me, and Spooken in the back seat and Daddy, Mother, and Gerald in the front.

Daddy pushed the black button to start the car. The engine made some noise but wouldn't start. Gerald got out, raised the hood, stuck his hand in, and jiggled something. He told Daddy to try again. The engine started and we headed out on the road. The last thing I remember seeing was Mother's washtub on the porch of the old farmhouse. We didn't have room for it in the trailer.

At almost five years of age, I couldn't imagine that another house would look any different from the one I'd known all my life, but when we arrived in Texarkana, I was astonished. Our house sat right near the road and behind it was a barn. Beyond the barn I could see a pond. It was beautiful.

Mother announced she would get a flock of chickens. When Amos arrived, Daddy could start plowing the ground to raise the bedding plants for the feed and seed store. There were enough bedrooms for everyone—one for Mother and Daddy, one for Barbara and me, and one for Gerald and Ben.

I couldn't wait to get everything moved in so I could explore the place. Things were going to be good here. All my fears disappeared.

2 TEXARKANA

I loved living in Texarkana. Most days I got up early and watched Daddy walk out to the barn to get Amos. Then he'd hook him to the plow and make long, straight rows. Sometimes Daddy let me walk in front of him, holding the handles of the plow. The plow turned up big, white grubs, and the earth felt warm and moist to my bare feet. When Daddy tired of me, he sent me back to the house, saying, "Get on outta here, Kay-Doll, you're in my way."

My brother Ben had started first grade. Since he was in school all day, I learned to entertain myself.

When Daddy wasn't in the field or at church, he could be found working on our old rattletrap car to keep it running. I played with my doll and my cats under the nearby shade tree. My cats were barn cats that I had coaxed into becoming pets. I loved to dress them in doll dresses and feed them milk from a little plastic doll's bottle.

Sometimes I heard grunting sounds and I'd look up. Daddy's head would be under the hood of the car, and he'd be holding a tool in his hand. If it was a loud grunt, his head would jerk from under the hood and he'd throw his tool as far down the road as he could. Pacing around the car, he'd say, "Dadgum the dadbum luck, this car ain't worth a dime. Kay-Doll, go down yonder and get my tool."

I dutifully trotted down the gravel road, found the tool, and brought it back to him. This happened almost every time he worked on the car. Then I went back to playing with my doll and my cats.

Mother had a big flock of chickens, which she called Leghorns. They were all white and they all looked the same to me. We had brought our dog Spooken with us from the Red River Valley. He was a brindle-colored pit bull that had been given to us as an eight-week-old puppy. Mother said his face looked like a spook, so she named him Spooken. She sang his praises and declared he was the smartest dog she ever had. She could point out one chicken and command Spooken to "go get it." The chickens scattered all over the chicken yard as Spooken ran straight into the flock, coming back with the exact chicken Mother had wanted, clutching it in his mouth.

Mother quickly wrung the chicken's neck, pulled out the entrails, and plunged it into a tub of hot water. It was my job to pluck the feathers. The big feathers were easy to pull out, but I struggled with the short little pin feathers. When I thought I was done, Mother examined the chicken.

"Kay," she said, dropping the "Doll" as she sometimes did, "you haven't finished plucking this chicken. You have to get the pin feathers out, too."

I resumed my plucking. I thought I was grown up enough to do everything Mother asked me to do.

By the time Ben finished the first grade, I was getting anxious to go to school myself. I began pestering Mother.

"How long will it be until I start school?" I asked her as she peeled sweet potatoes. Mother put down the peeling knife and fixed me with a piercing look.

"You won't be going to school here. We'll be moving."

I stared at her, not knowing what to say, as usual. My words stuck in my throat, and I felt that familiar tornado inside my head, blotting out the questions I couldn't ask.

It turned out that Daddy had heard God call on him to preach the Gospel. I wondered how God did it. Did he come right down from heaven, walk into the house, and call out to Daddy to come and listen to him? Maybe he sent an angel down to tell him. Daddy prayed a lot, but I couldn't imagine how God talked back to him, because I had never seen or heard God in our house.

The place we were heading next was called Walnut Ridge, Arkansas. Daddy had applied to Bible college there. It was a dream for him, and it had taken hard work to achieve that dream. Both Daddy and Mother had been forced to quit school after the eighth grade to help their families in the fields. A high school diploma was a requirement for Bible college, so Daddy found out how to get a book so he could learn all the subjects and pass the test. He was so proud when he completed everything and the certificate came in the mail. (Daddy kept that book, and when I was older, I looked through it and was amazed by all the information it contained that Daddy had memorized, including French and Spanish.)

Going to Bible college might have been a dream for Daddy, but I didn't understand why we couldn't stay where we already had a church.

Our social activities in Texarkana had been centered around the Southern Baptist church we attended several times a week. Sunday mornings, Sunday evenings, Wednesday night prayer meetings—we were in attendance, rain or shine. The grownups studied the scripture and prayed while Ben and I attended classes.

Ben was a member of the Royal Ambassadors and I studied with the Girls Auxiliary. I hated that name. Girls Auxiliary! Why couldn't *we* have the word "Royal" in the name of our group. It didn't seem fair.

The mission of the classes was to turn Ben and me into good ambassadors for Christ. I liked the stories and the pictures, but I didn't understand the Bible verses I had to memorize.

After church on Sunday, Daddy sometimes invited company to come home with us and have dinner. After dinner, everyone went out on the porch for some "bluegrass music." Daddy played the banjo, Mother the harmonica, and guests might play either a fiddle or guitar. One man who played fiddle had a crooked leg and walked funny. I liked him because he always paid attention to me and made me laugh. I felt sorry that he had such a hard time walking, so I often prayed that Jesus would heal his leg. In spite of my prayers, he wasn't healed. I had been told that prayers were answered, but I began to suspect that the stories in the Bible might be mostly made up.

Now we were leaving Texarkana, where I had been so happy, and I couldn't make sense of the reason. It was just like the move from the Red River Valley—confusing and scary.

I tried to imagine the next house. I thought that maybe it would be like the one we were leaving. I heard the word "Arkansas," but I didn't know what it meant. I somehow got the idea from listening to Daddy talk to Uncle Marshall that it was far away.

When the time came, I didn't want to get into my Uncle Marshall's big flatbed lumber truck. I clutched my two dolls close to my heart and began to cry. As I stood sniffling with tears in my eyes, I felt the cool morning air and heard the hum of the cicadas as they began their daily flight. I dug my bare feet into the dirt and felt as if my happy memories were floating away with the echo of the cicadas as they disappeared in the distance.

Mother interrupted my thoughts. "There's no room for those dolls nor the doll bed," she announced.

I cried louder and clutched my dolls tighter.

Uncle Marshall intervened. "Oh, Mary," he said to my mother, "we can make room for the dolls. We'll leave the doll bed. It's just an old orange crate, anyway."

"Okay, but we can't take Spooken, either," she replied. "He'll have to stay with Uncle Fred until we come back and get him."

I didn't dare cry about the dog or the doll bed, because I knew Mother would slap me and tell me to "shut up or I'll give you something to cry about." Mother hadn't smiled or laughed in days.

The rest of the family climbed into the cab of my uncle's truck. Uncle Marshall, Daddy, Mother, my brother Ben, and I were crammed in like sardines. My brother Gerald and sister Barbara followed us in a friend's car that was loaded down with more of our belongings.

As I gazed at the house we were leaving, my stomach felt as if a cold, hard hand was squeezing my insides. I saw one of my cats come out to the yard and look at us and felt like I was shattering into pieces. I hadn't had a chance to kiss and hug her goodbye.

My uncle grabbed the gearshift sticking out of the floor and ground it into gear. The hand in my stomach clenched tighter as the truck rolled onto the road. I knew I would never play with my cats again. Who would I love on and sing little songs to?

I had no way of knowing that life in Arkansas would turn out to be very different from the poor but pleasant life I had enjoyed in Texas.

Daddy, Kay, Mother and Ben

Mother at Age 19

Kay, Ben and Puppies

3 ARKANSAS

As we made our way to Walnut Ridge, we stopped periodically for gas. Ben and I were allowed to jump out of the truck and run around for a few minutes. We were amazed by all the sights in the small towns we had never seen before. I saw a building in one town with a big sign, and people were lining up outside, waiting to go inside.

"What's that?" I asked Mother, pointing to the building. "Why are all the people in line?"

"It's a place for picture shows," she said. I took the risk of making her mad by asking a second question. "What's a picture show?"

"It's a place where people go to watch a story by looking at pictures."

I didn't know what that meant, but when we got back in the truck, I tried to imagine what a picture show might look like. I thought it would probably be about all my cats and dogs and the funny things they did. Mostly it would be about what I did every day.

We drove the entire day. The truck was stifling hot the whole time and I couldn't move without aggravating everyone in the cab. At one point Mother said, "If you don't be still, I'm gonna slap the fire outta you." The more I tried to be still, the more I desperately needed to move. Ben was wedged between Uncle Marshall and me. Nobody said *he* couldn't move and every time he did, my desperation grew. I finally leaned way forward, then back again. Mother grabbed me by the hair, saying, "I told you to be still!" She pulled my hair so hard it made my eyes tear up. Ben jabbed me with his elbow and when I looked at him, he had a smile on his face because I had gotten in trouble. I wanted to slap that smile right off, but I knew I couldn't.

After about ten hours, my uncle stopped the truck by rows of old red buildings. I was relieved that we were finally there. There were front doors all along the buildings, with a couple of steps leading up to each door. I asked Daddy what the buildings were, and he said they were old military barracks from World War II. I asked, "What's a barrack? Are we going to live in them?"

"Yes, we are," he said, "And you're looking at them."

I still wondered why they didn't look like regular houses, the ones I had seen all my life, but I figured his answer was all I was going to get from him. We walked into one of the doors and Daddy and my uncle brought our belongings inside.

As I looked around the rest of the rooms we were to live in, I had a dark feeling. I went outside and looked around. The barrack was long, with several other apartments, and everywhere I looked I saw nothing but dirt and weeds. There were no trees, just more barracks. Ben came over and said, "I don't like this place, do you?" I shook my head and wondered where Ben and I could play. Would there be other children to play with? It sure didn't look like it to me.

I followed my big sister Barbara out of the apartment and down some stairs to where the bathroom was located. We were to share this bathroom with the neighbors who lived in the apartment on each side of ours. Barbara showed me the string I had to pull to turn on the naked light bulb in the middle of the ceiling. I had to jump twice to reach it. Light flooded the basement and cockroaches scattered in every direction towards the corners of the big room, looking for a dark place to hide. The word "evil" suddenly darted into my mind. It smelled evil and dank.

I grabbed Barbara and begged her not to make me go in there.

"They're just cockroaches," she said. "They won't hurt you."

"Yes, they will," I whimpered, backing out of the room, pulling her with me. There were several toilets, sinks, and showers. I had always bathed in a washtub and I had never seen a shower before. I knew I didn't want to get in there. The cockroaches were sure to run over my feet. I made Barbara promise to go down to the bathroom with me if she was home.

I'll never forget the first time I had to use the bathroom when Barbara wasn't home. It was still daylight, so I convinced myself I wasn't scared as I walked down the stairs. I jumped up and pulled the string and the basement lit up. I settled on the toilet with my bare feet on the cement floor. No cockroaches in sight. Suddenly I looked down and saw a cockroach crawling straight toward my feet. He had been hiding behind the toilet. I screamed, jerked my feet up, and nearly fell off the toilet. Pulling my panties up and running up the stairs as fast as I could, I ran straight to my mother.

"Well," she said when I told her what happened, "maybe you should put your shoes on before going down to use the bathroom."

It doesn't matter, I thought, not daring to say it out loud, because I'm never going to go down there again.

In Walnut Ridge Barbara and I shared a bed, as we always had. Many nights I dreamed I was in the old farmhouse in Texarkana. In my dream I was sitting on the toilet. I felt warmth touch my body, and the next thing I knew, Barbara was shaking me angrily. "Kay-Doll, you're peeing the bed!" she yelled. As she pulled the sheets off the bed, she reminded me that I hadn't peed the bed before and demanded to know why I was doing it now.

"I don't know," I whispered. I didn't have the words to tell her that in my dream I was sitting on the toilet. I had visions of cockroaches swarming around my feet. "I'm afraid to go down there."

Finally, my sister started making sure I went to the bathroom with her just before going to bed. The bedwetting stopped.

My brother Ben was a tough, wiry little guy with steely blue eyes, not much taller than I was but determined to let me know about once a week that he was still taller. He was always on the go and looking for something to do. He never backed down from a fight or any chance to get into mischief.

We didn't know any of the other kids in the area yet, and we were used to playing by ourselves since we had lived in the country in Texas. The small Bible college was on a closed-down military base a few miles outside Walnut Ridge. About a mile from the barracks, we found a place where old World War II bombers were parked. A couple of helicopters were also parked on a nearby airstrip.

Ben was in his element, and I tagged along.

Two men were working on the helicopters. Ben immediately started asking questions and found out the men owned them.

"How do you fly that thing?" he asked. "Can you show me how?"

Within ten minutes Ben and the men had struck a deal. Ben and I would wash their helicopters and they would take us up for a ride.

We got busy, washing like crazy. At six and seven years old, I'm not sure how well we did the job, but we gave it our best efforts. We were both agile as spiders and could climb anything. Ben was on top of the helicopter in a flash with his soapy rag, washing as hard as he could.

"Kay, get up here with your rag and help me!"

Our hard work paid off. One of the men said, "Okie, dokie. You'all climb in."

I wasn't tall enough to climb up, so he gave me a boost. After getting us settled, he climbed in and started the engine. The big blades started turning and spun faster and faster. The helicopter started going straight up, leaving the ground. I was scared and couldn't hear a thing for all the noise. The blades were whirling around faster and faster. From where I was sitting, I saw the tips fly by. Pretty soon they were just a blur. I couldn't hear anything except my own heart thumping in my ears.

It was fascinating to look down and see the barracks, looking like little toy houses all strung together. I saw tiny people, no bigger than Ben and me, walking around. I waved like crazy and called to them, "Hey, look up and look at me!"

I didn't know they couldn't see or hear me. Ben was in the seat next to the pilot, earphones on his head, begging to steer the plane, push some buttons, or pull some levers. I imagine that's when Ben fell in love with flying.

Every day that summer we got up, ate cold biscuits, and told Mother we were headed for the base. If the men weren't there, we just wandered into the old World War II planes. We pretended we were flying them and dropping bombs, shouting commands at each other as we sat in the cockpit.

"See that? Drop the bomb!"

"I'll drop two! BAM!"

When we grew tired of dropping imaginary bombs, we dug empty bullet shells out of mounds of dirt that had been used for target practice during the war. We used the shells for whistles, and we soon discovered that the bigger the shell, the better it whistled. The bigger shells made a deeper sound than the smaller ones.

One day Ben found an unexploded shell and took it home. He set it on the shelf of the gas cookstove and forgot about it.

We were awakened the next morning by a loud bang, followed by the sound of our mother screaming. We jumped out of our beds and ran to the kitchen. Mother was standing in her flannel nightgown with blood running down her face and one of her hands. I watched as Daddy helped her get dressed so he could take her to see the doctor. The dress was red and white, and it occurred to me that if the blood dripped on the red part of the dress, it wouldn't show.

I began to cry and shake. I felt that familiar cold, hard hand clench my empty stomach and it hurt. I was terrified Mother might die.

Since we didn't have a car, a neighbor took her to the Bible college infirmary. When Mother came home, she had a large bandage on her forehead and another on her hand. "After Daddy lit the oven for me to cook the biscuits, I picked up that hot bullet, then I dropped it," she said. The bullet had exploded, and she had been struck by shrapnel.

I thanked God that my mother was still alive.

We didn't get a whipping for bringing that bullet home. Nobody said we couldn't go to the airfield and play, so we continued going there every day. We just made sure that the bullet casings we dug up were empty, so nobody would get hurt.

Fearless Ben was always looking for something exciting to do. Today he would have been pegged with attention deficit hyperactivity disorder (ADHD).

The two of us could be away from home all day without any supervision. We were roaming around one day when Ben saw a bat hanging upside down in a tree. He immediately seized on the idea that both of us should climb up the tree and knock the bat down. He got there first and promptly knocked the bat out of the tree. It landed on my head. The bat clung to my hair and I screamed, grabbing hold of it with both hands and squeezing as I fell out of the tree.

We ran all the way home. When we burst into the house, Mother pried my hands loose and threw what was left of the bat out the door.

"Kay," she admonished sternly. "Now I have to put coal oil on your head to keep you from getting rabies, and I'm gonna have to shave the top of your head!"

I howled and flailed my arms to get away from her. She finally gave in and agreed not to shave my head.

Ben jumped up and down, yelling, "Is she gonna die? Is she gonna die?" The thought that I might die hadn't occurred to me, but now it made me yell even louder.

"Shut up, Ben!" Mother said. "She's not going to die. Not from this, anyway!"

The smell of the coal oil made me want to throw up. I refused to go outside the rest of the day with coal oil in my hair, so I sat in my bedroom with my head hanging down, waiting for Barbara to come home from school. I knew *she* would feel sorry for me.

Most of my childhood injuries could be traced to my brother Ben. The incident with the bat was soon followed by another frightening "adventure."

Ben had spotted a hornet's nest under the eve of a building. I warned him to leave it alone, but he ignored me as usual. Instead, he took a long stick and knocked the nest down. Swarms of hornets flew out, and one stung me right between the eyes. Other hornets stung me on my arms and legs. By the time I got home, running all the way, my eyes were already swollen shut. Mother grabbed me and starting scolding both of us as she dabbed vinegar everywhere I had been stung.

Of course Ben claimed it was my own fault, not his. I

had stood too close to where the nest landed, he declared.

Once Ben and I were waiting for Mother and Daddy as they attended a church meeting. We were told to stay in the car as they wouldn't be long. We sat in the car for a while, watching other kids playing outside.

"C'mon, let's go play," Ben said as he got out of the car. I followed right behind him. I was standing behind him when something caught his attention and he threw his head back to look up at the sky, breaking my nose in the process. Mother and Daddy were furious, and the next day my eyes were black and blue and swollen shut. The injury caused a bump in my nose that I had to live with the rest of my life.

Ben and I spent the rest of our first summer in Arkansas roaming around and getting into mischief. I had several scars to show for that summer, but all the incidents with my brother also served to toughen me up. It was a quality I would need in the years ahead.

Starting our new life was hard on everyone in the family. Daddy had a job as a night watchman on the campus of the Bible college, and he returned from work in the morning just in time to see my brother Gerald head out on his paper route before going to school. Both Gerald and Barbara were still in high school, but we needed the money Gerald could earn.

Food was scarce. There was no place for Mother to plant a garden, or to keep a flock of chickens or a cow, so we mostly ate water gravy and biscuits and potatoes. If God had seen fit to answer Daddy's prayers about Bible college, I wondered, why didn't He tell us how to get food? After about six months my weight was down to thirty-five pounds, much too thin for six years of age. I was too tired to walk, and one day the neighbor lady said, "Kay, you ain't no bigger than a slat."

Mother became worried to the point where she asked the neighbor to drive us to the doctor. I was scared, since I hadn't been to a doctor before, but I was also interested in what he was doing. Why was he putting this cold hard thing against my chest, and what were those long black hoses that ran up to his ears? He stood still, quietly listening, before he put the hoses down and asked my mother, "What does she eat? Does she eat three times a day?"

I could tell Mother didn't want to admit that we ate biscuits and water gravy three times a day. Finally, the doctor said, "Mrs. Runyan, this girl needs to eat some fruits and vegetables."

I saw Mother's body go rigid. She was too ashamed to tell him we didn't have any fruits and vegetables, nor did we have the money to buy them.

Later that day, as we were eating supper, I pushed away the biscuit with gravy and began whining about fruit.

Mother slapped me so hard I fell off my chair.

My sister Barbara jumped up and yelled at her. "Stop it!" As she reached down to help me up, Mother jumped on her and pushed her down to the floor. Pulling Barbara's hair, she yelled, "Don't you dare tell me what to do!"

The pressure of seeing her family go hungry had caused Mother to snap. She had no way of making things better and she knew it. The frustration, guilt, and shame were taking their toll.

Soon Daddy began to cough, continually bringing up nasty, green stuff from his lungs. He stayed in bed most days and was unable to attend Bible classes or work at his night watchman job. I was afraid he might be dying. Gerald took over the night watchman job, adding that responsibility to his paper route and attending high school. He was only able to sleep for a few hours after school, so he quickly became exhausted. Mother ordered Ben and me to go outside and play until supper, so we wouldn't disturb Gerald.

Sometimes a little girl who lived a few doors down from us sat outside on the stairs, eating an apple or some other snack. I tortured myself by staring at her as she ate, while my own stomach growled with hunger. By the time Ben and I went in for supper, Mother didn't have to worry that I wouldn't eat my biscuits and gravy.

Daddy eventually went to the infirmary and was diagnosed with walking pneumonia. The doctor prescribed medication that enabled him to return to Bible college and his night watchman job. We were all glad Gerald could give up that job, as he had been driven to the point of complete exhaustion.

The fit of temper Mother had displayed after the doctor told her to feed me fruits and vegetables was not an isolated incident. She had come from a family where violence was commonplace, and whenever she was pushed to her limit or felt she was being backed into a corner, she resorted to the physical violence she grew up with. Sometimes she took her anger out on Daddy. One morning she got into an argument with him and jumped up from the table, yelling, "I'll just knock your old head off!" With that she took a swing at him, catching him on the neck. Gerald pulled her off Daddy, who just said, "Well, Mary!" as if he were surprised. He never fought back, just said, "Well, Mary!" every time it happened.

Mother had no qualms about whipping Ben or me with a belt if we misbehaved. If Barbara tried to take the belt away, Mother would turn on her, too. The only person who ever escaped her wrath was Gerald. She thought of him as the real provider for the family, even though he was only sixteen years old.

When I was older, I learned more about Mother's family—how one of her older brothers had beaten his wife to death with the butt of a rifle, how her other brothers had beaten their wives and children, and how even her little sister had nearly killed a boy in a fight when she was just twelve years old. Mother used the same coping skills that had been used on her when she was growing up.

The best way to deal with her anger was to avoid

making her mad in the first place, something I wasn't always able to do.

By the time summer was over, I was excited about starting first grade. I had begged Ben all summer long to teach me how to count to one hundred and how to say my "ABCs." He was willing to tell me how to do both, but too impatient to sit and let me say them back to him. "I bet you can't remember what I just said," he'd taunt me. Thankfully, Barbara let me practice with her when she was at home.

I couldn't wait for school to start. I just knew that I would know more than anybody else in my class.

I walked to school with Ben, happy as I could be that I was finally old enough to go to school. My mother had registered me as "Kay," so "Kay-Doll" was now reserved for use by family, another sign that I was grown up now. The only shadow over my happiness was the gnawing hunger in my stomach. "Drink water from the drinking fountain, as much as you can, and you won't feel so hungry," Ben told me. I figured he must be right about that. After all, he had already been going to school for a while.

Our school was a three-room schoolhouse and accommodated first through twelfth grades. I was assigned to the same room as Ben and the others who had finished the first grade. When the teacher called on me to count to one hundred, I was proud of myself since I didn't make a single mistake. Surely the other kids would be in awe of my intelligence.

Now it was time to write. After a few minutes, the teacher walked over to my desk and stopped. I glanced up to find her looking at me, unsmiling. She reached down, took my pencil from my left hand, and placed it in my right hand. I was confused and too timid to ask her why she did that. She didn't do that to anyone else. My face felt hot when I realized I had been writing with the wrong hand. How could I be so stupid? I just knew without looking that the other kids were staring at me. I tried to make the letters and numbers with my right hand, like everyone else, but they looked like what Mother called "chicken scratching."

Now I knew I wasn't as smart as the other kids, after all. I glanced over at the girl next to me and saw that her paper didn't look anything like mine. I hunched over so no one could see what I was doing, and when I turned in my paper, I just hoped the teacher would be able to read my name.

I didn't feel excited about school any more.

Years later I learned from my sister that the teacher had talked to my mother. "Mrs. Runyan," she said, "Kay is a *leftie*. Do you want me to teach her how to write with her right hand?"

Mother thought about this for a minute. "Well," she said in her practical way, "it's a right-handed world, so maybe you should teach her to write with her right hand."

I became ambidextrous, using my left hand for many things, but I always wrote with my right hand after that. I was never very proud of my report cards, especially all the Cs in penmanship.

I wished my handwriting had been the only thing that prevented me from fitting in with the other kids in my class, but it wasn't.

When the weather started to turn colder, Mother went to the donation center at the Bible college and picked out shoes for Ben and me. Mine were too big, and I showed her.

"Be happy with what you got. There weren't a lot of choices. You'll grow into them."

I could barely walk in those shoes. I had to curl my toes down to keep them from coming off my feet. Barbara noticed this and put some soft cloth in the toes of each shoe. I thought this would solve the problem and I wouldn't have to be embarrassed any more, but during recess, while jumping rope with the other kids, my shoe flew off my foot.

One of the girls ran up and said, "Hey, those were my shoes!"

Everyone laughed. I hung my head and walked away, carrying my shoe and stuffing the rag back in the toe.

Just when school was about to end for the summer, Mother told me that we were moving back to Texas. Daddy had finished his training at the Bible college but becoming a minister would not happen immediately. He and Mother had gotten jobs in Hart, Texas. I was happy, because I didn't like being hungry and I didn't like school.

I couldn't wait to leave Arkansas.

4 THE HIGH PLAINS

It was Uncle Ed who had recommended that Daddy contact the principal of the school in Hart, Texas, about working there. The principal hired Daddy to drive the school bus and hired Mother to cook in the school cafeteria. All I could think about was that I hoped we would have enough food to eat when we moved to a different place.

On the way to Hart, we had to stop and retrieve our dog, Spooken. We had left him with Daddy's brother, Uncle Fred, when we moved to Arkansas. There was only one problem—Uncle Fred didn't want to give Spooken back. "He's my dog now and you can't have him," he told Mother. "Best cow dog I ever had."

We were staying with Mother's sister, Aunt Ruby, who lived across the woods from Fred. "Spooken's going with us to west Texas," Mother vowed. "Fred may think he's keeping my dog, but he's got another thought coming." She had a plan, and I knew nothing was going to stop her, because she had that look where her mouth was like a pencil line across her face and her blue eyes had taken on a hard expression. "C'mon, Kay-Doll, let's go," she said, insisting that Aunt Ruby and I go with her to get Spooken back.

I was afraid. I had heard stories about Uncle Fred getting drunk, going into town, and threatening to shoot anybody who crossed him. He was constantly feuding with Aunt Ruby and her husband. One time, after yet another property dispute, Fred drove over to their cow pasture and backed his pickup truck right up to the fence. Then he tied a rope to the gate and dragged that gate down Main Street so Aunt Ruby's husband Sandy, who was inside the coffee shop, could see what he had done. Half of Ruby and Sandy's cows were soon wandering down the road. For good measure, Fred also punched Sandy in the face. I knew I had good reason to fear Uncle Fred.

Mother, Aunt Ruby, and I started walking through the pine trees and underbrush toward Uncle Fred's place. The brush scratched my legs. "I wanna go back," I whined. "Fred's gonna shoot us."

"Shut up and be quiet," Mother said, "because if he hears us, he just might shoot us."

"Yeah, he ain't got a lick of sense," added Ruby.

As we got closer, we could see his shack through the trees. I looked around for bigger trees that I might be able to hide behind if he pulled out his shotgun. I had touched some of the trees and I smelled the sap on my hands, which were now sticky. This area of east Texas was known as the "piney woods" for good reason.

I wanted to turn around and run back to Aunt Ruby's house, but just then Mother put two fingers to her mouth and whistled. Our dog Spooken came running. He remembered her whistle! He jumped into her arms, almost knocking Mother backwards. He was so skinny and starved-looking that I suspected he'd only gotten scraps to eat, whatever was left after Fred's seven kids finished their plates.

We headed back to Ruby's house and left for the high plains of west Texas early the next morning.

Years later I found out that Uncle Fred had been furious

when he arrived home to find Spooken gone. He had grabbed his shotgun, but his wife and kids made him put the gun down. He still intended to get the dog back, but we left before he had a chance.

We all got up at four o'clock and drove the entire day. My brother Gerald's nose bled most of the way, for some reason. By the time we arrived, every wash cloth and towel in the car was soaked in blood.

As we drove into the little town of Hart, Texas, I saw a small grocery store, a dime store, and a gas station. Daddy stopped a man walking outside the grocery store and asked him where the Baptist church was.

"Down yonder," the man said, pointing the way.

"Thanks. We need to get this boy some help and find a house to live in."

Staring out the open window, all I could see from the car was flat land, red sand, tumbleweeds, cotton, and alfalfa fields. Tractors plowed here and there, followed by clouds of dust. The hot air blew into my face and the air felt different from what I was used to. I was scared there wouldn't be a place for us to live.

Hart was a small farming town with a population of about two hundred fifty people. There weren't any vacant houses, but the principal said he could have a house fixed up for us to move into before school started. In the meantime, we moved in with my Uncle Ed and his family.

Uncle Ed's five kids were not church-goers, and they thought Ben and I needed to learn a few things about grown-up pleasures.

"Let's go smoke a cigarette," my cousin Gary said one day as Ben and I played outside.

"Why?" we asked in unison, stunned.

Gary laughed and said, "What? You ain't never smoked?"

I had been taught that smoking was a sin, but the idea intrigued me. Gary knew where to find his daddy's cigarettes, and soon we were all sitting behind the cattle watering tank, out of sight of the house. I watched all my cousins smoke and listened closely when they told me what to do. I took a draw on an unfiltered Camel cigarette and inhaled the smoke like they said, but my head immediately started spinning and I began coughing. I stumbled back to the house with the warning that I'd better not tell. I felt sick, and Mother couldn't figure out what was wrong. She must have had her suspicions, though, because she kept asking me what I had done. I was afraid to tell her because I didn't think I could take a whipping. I was already feeling the worst I had ever felt. I spent the rest of the day lying in bed with my stomach roiling.

I knew God was going to punish me because smoking was a sin. My body was a temple of God and I wasn't supposed to defile it in any way. That's what the ministers had preached over and over again. "Please God," I prayed. "Don't punish me anymore, and I will never defile my body again."

As it turned out, my cousin Ronnie Mac got the whipping. Uncle Ed figured out that his cigarettes were disappearing at a rapid rate. Somehow the blame landed on Ronnie, my cousin. Uncle Ed started taking off his belt as he grabbed Ronnie by the arm, yelling, "I'm gonna give you a whooping you won't forget!"

And he did. I kept thinking Uncle Ed would stop hitting Ronnie with his belt, but he kept on until my other cousin started yelling for him to stop and tried to get between his dad and brother. We all felt sorry for Ronnie Mac and sat with him behind the house as we watched the red welts come out on his legs and back.

My smoking days were over.

Before long Uncle Ed heard that a farmer was moving into a new house he had built. It was decided that Uncle Ed's family would move into the farmer's old house and we would stay in the one we were living in until school started. The house had no electricity and we had to use lamps that burned a clear oil.

Before my uncle's family moved out, Aunt Dollie Mae, Ed's wife, had helped with the laundry, but now I was not to be spared that chore. To wash clothes, Mother built a fire in the yard and heated water in a big iron tub. I had the job of stirring the clothes with a long stick that had a paddle on the end. The fire was hot and sweat poured down my face as I stirred the clothes. Then I ladled each piece of clothing into a rinse tub. Mother and I wrung them out and hung them on the clothesline to dry. After that Mother heated the iron on the wood cookstove and she and Barbara ironed the clothes.

The high plains of Texas have unbearably hot summers. Most days there wasn't a hint of a breeze, and to make matters worse, we had to build a fire in the stove to heat the iron and to cook.

Somehow we all survived it, though. We knew it was temporary. Just before school started, we were able to move into the house on the school grounds. Electricity and an indoor toilet! I was thrilled that I would no longer have to dodge the tarantulas that had lurked around Uncle Ed's outdoor toilet. Sleeping in a rollaway bed in the living room was a tradeoff I was more than willing to make.

The house was next door to the school. The principal lived on the other side of our place. He was a tall, rail thin man who seldom spoke. He attended the Catholic church in the next town, even though his wife, like our family, went to the Baptist church. Daddy referred to him as "*that Catholic*," so I stayed as far away from him as I could, even though I didn't know what a "Catholic" was. I wasn't sure what he might do to me, him being a Catholic and all.

My mother had to leave the house early in the morning because she was the school cook. I was left on my own to figure out what to wear, so I picked out a dress Mother had made for me out of a flour sack. Whenever we bought flour, I tried to pick out a flour sack that had flowers on it because I knew eventually it would become a dress for me. This flour sack had little blue flowers on it, and I thought it would be pretty.

When I saw the dresses the other girls were wearing to school, I felt a deep sense of shame about my flour sack dress. This was not the way I had hoped to start out in this school.

On the second day of school, I made an enemy. My second-grade teacher, Miss Jewell Scott, noticed I had gotten up onto my knees on my desk chair so that I could see the blackboard better. She had put me in the very back row.

"Sit down, you little Arkie!" she said with a piercing look that seared my soul. "Don't you have any manners?"

Everyone turned around and stared at me. I felt the blood rush to my face, making it hot. I imagined my freckles stood out like warts, and the thought entered my mind that maybe I had forgotten to brush my hair that morning.

I slid down into my chair. Yesterday I thought her name was pretty. I had never heard of anyone named Jewell. I had admired her black hair, flashing black eyes, and red lipstick. Now her name was as ugly as she was.

At recess I watched enviously as the other girls jumped rope. It was my favorite thing to do during recess, but as I approached them, my courage drained right out of my head and oozed out through my feet. I turned and scuffed my shoes into the red dirt, glancing down at my homemade dress.

Miss Jewell Scott was so stupid, she didn't even know I was born in Texas and had only lived in Arkansas for a year and a half. How dare she hurt my feelings like that. I wanted revenge and when I told my brother Ben what had happened, he became my willing accomplice.

"Well, she'll pay for that," he declared.

The next Saturday morning we waited in the field near Jewell Scott's house until we were certain she'd left for town. Her freshly washed laundry hung on the clothesline in her yard—white girdles, white underpants, and white slips. Ben and I found an empty bucket and filled it half full with red sand and dirt, adding water to make mud balls. My heart was beating fast. I knew we'd get a good whipping if Mother found out what we were doing, but she and Daddy were in town, too.

I picked up the first mud ball, rolled it around in my hands, and threw it at Jewell's clean laundry. I was a good shot, hitting a white slip right in the middle. The mud formed a round brown spot before slowly dripping down her slip in long, reddish-brown squiggly lines. Now my heart was really pounding. I threw another mud ball. *Splat!* I hit her bra and it fell to the ground, red and muddy. Ben was having his own fun, throwing one mud ball after the other.

"Take that!" we yelled. "This is what you get, you old witch!"

I was sure that I heard Ben say "bitch." I didn't know that word, but I knew it was bad.

We were Southern Baptists so we couldn't use real curse words. We had to be satisfied with "witch," "ugly witch," "fatty," and "stupid." Daddy said if he ever heard a curse word coming out of our mouths, he would box our jaws good. When we ran out of mud balls, I was ready to go because I thought we had done a good job of messing up her clothes.

"C'mon, Ben, let's go."

"I wanna get that girdle," he said.

He managed to make one more mud ball and threw it hard enough to knock the girdle off the clothesline and into the dirt. We ran home lickety split, laughing all the way because every single one of Jewell Scott's undergarments lay on the ground, splattered with mud.

We never got caught. I felt good, but I knew I had been wicked. God was probably going to punish me and put a check mark beside my name in the big black book He kept. I pushed that thought aside as I ran into the house, sat on the couch, and laughed again as I thought about Jewell coming home and discovering what we'd done. If I could just get through second grade, I'd never have to see that witch again.

Lo and behold, my hopes were dashed when I learned that Jewell Scott was going to be teaching *third* grade. I decided to lay low and never open my mouth unless she called on me. I tried hard to do all my lessons, but she mostly gave me Cs. I knew it was only because she thought I was from Arkansas. If she knew I was a Texan, I'd have gotten As or Bs for sure.

One night as we all lay sleeping, our dog, Spooken, began to growl. Daddy got out of bed and headed to the kitchen, where he was shocked to see flames reflected through the pulled-down window shade. Spooken hadn't been growling after all. The sound came from boiling water in our pipes, which connected to the pipes in the school. The school was burning down.

Soon Daddy was moving the school bus, Mother was backing our car out of the driveway, and Gerald was hosing down our house. I briefly wondered if our house would burn down, too, but more than that, I wondered if the school burning down meant I would finally be free of Jewell Scott.

No such luck. A week later Army barracks were moved onto the school grounds so we'd have classrooms. I walked into my class and there she was. Black hair, black eyes, and those red, red lips. I was doomed.

I dragged myself to school every day, slinking into Jewell's class, sitting in the back row where she had told me I had to sit, and praying for summer.

No one ever figured out how the fire started.

After school, Ben and I picked cotton alongside the Mexican kids who swam the Rio Grande in order to pick cotton, too. It was back-breaking work, but at least I was doing it with a full stomach. Since Mother was the school cook, she brought home leftover food every day. It was the first time I remembered having plenty to eat. Daddy was still driving the school bus. Life was hard but we had some stability.

In spite of Miss Jewell Scott, I didn't want to leave Hart. Mother, however didn't like the high plains, the blowing red sand, and the fact that you couldn't see one little hill with trees. "The only hill you can see in this godforsaken place is an ant hill, swarming with red fire ants," she complained.

Daddy had heard that Oregon was the place to be. *The land of milk and honey.* Soon we were on the move again.

Kay in Second Grade

Kay in Third Grade

5 OREGON

It was our own *Grapes of Wrath* journey. I was ten years old when we set out for Oregon in 1953. No jobs were waiting this time for Mother or Daddy, so we were relying on Daddy's faith. We loaded up our two-wheel trailer and Daddy, Mother, and Gerald piled into the front seat of our 1947 Ford. Ben, our two dogs, Spooken and Smokey Joe (our new pit bull), and I were crammed into the back seat. My sister Barbara remained behind in Texas since she had a job working for the telephone company in Amarillo.

We drove for three days and nights, stopping only to buy bologna and bread and use the gas station bathrooms. By the time we finally reached Oregon's McKenzie Pass, the car was in bad shape. The winter snow was melting in the mountains, and water was coming up into the floor of the car. Ben and I tried to hold our feet up to avoid the freezing cold water. The engine kept vapor-locking and overheating. Gerald filled an empty Coke bottle with water from one of the many waterfalls next to the road and poured it into the radiator.

"These mountains are pulling the guts out of this car," he warned.

We were all feeling the stress and strain of this trip. Mother was wedged between Daddy and Gerald in the front seat, and she had been carrying a lampshade on her lap the entire journey. Gerald was driving. At one point Daddy, who was drifting in and out of sleep, thought Gerald was going off the road. He lunged for the steering wheel, putting both arms right through Mother's lampshade. I don't think Mother ever forgave him for that.

I had never seen so much water in my life. Waterfalls ran down the hills on each side of the road, and everything smelled clean and new. I loved the smell of the forest and the damp soil, so different from the dry red dirt of west Texas.

The exhaustion we all felt even extended to our two pit bulls. Ben and I didn't make it any easier, scaring the dogs with our fighting. I couldn't wait to get to a destination— anywhere would be fine with me.

We got as far as Eugene, Oregon, before the money ran out. We found an old, rundown house to rent. We gave the man who owned the house most of what we had in the trailer for the first month's rent. Daddy and Gerald found jobs working in a sawmill fifty miles away. They stayed there all week and came home on the weekend with food.

One of the neighbors had a cherry tree and Mother asked if we could pick some cherries. I had never tasted anything so sweet. I savored having that taste in my mouth until I fell asleep. Those first few days all we had to eat were cherries served over rice, but I knew better than to complain. I had no wish to be slapped by Mother and told to be thankful for what we had. She started digging up a small plot of dirt to plant a garden.

Another neighbor told Mother that she was going to donate blood for twenty-five dollars. Mother asked to go along. She felt God had answered her prayers and told Ben and me she'd buy us new shoes. I was excited about being able to start school wearing new shoes.

When the neighbor picked us up, Mother nervously asked her what it was like to have blood drawn. The lady assured her there was nothing to it. It was like getting a shot. Ben and I waited in the car until Mother and the lady finally returned. Her mouth was pulled down into a frown and I could tell by the way she walked that something was wrong.

"I'm sorry, Mary," the neighbor said as they were getting into the car.

"Mother, what happened?" I asked in a quiet voice.

She choked out the words. "My blood pressure was too high so they wouldn't take my blood."

I didn't know what "blood pressure" was, but I could see Mother was about to cry so I didn't ask. When we got home, she said, "I guess I worked myself into a tizzy about the whole thing."

It was the weekend and I couldn't wait for Gerald and Daddy to come home with food. Gerald surprised me and Ben by giving each of us a Snickers candy bar. I was in heaven. I rolled the chocolate around in my mouth for as long as I could without swallowing and savored the taste. I closed my eyes and felt like my head was in the clouds. Just as I opened my eyes, our dog Spooken jumped up and grabbed what was left of my Snickers and swallowed it whole, paper and all. I was crushed, but then I felt sorry for Spooken. He and Smokey Joe were as hungry as we were, living on the meager scraps we were able to give them.

A few days later Mother said, "We have to get rid of one of the dogs. We can only feed one of them." She told Ben and me that we had to choose and we had to do it right then. I couldn't speak. I could only stare at Mother and Ben as they decided Smokey Joe had to go. Ben fought back tears, and I knew Mother was desperate because she loved the dogs as much as Ben and I.

Mother said we'd drop Smokey Joe off at the dump because he would be able to find scraps of food there. We knew better than to argue with her and climbed into the car. Usually Smokey Joe loved to ride in the car, but this time he was hesitant. I held him on my lap and tried not to cry as I began to get a sick feeling in my stomach. I laid my head on his head and stroked his bony ribs as I breathed in his dog smell, hoping he knew I loved him. Ben sat beside me, not saying a word. I didn't dare look at him.

I could see the back of Mother's neck and head as she drove. Her short black hair had the usual waves in it that she made with her fingers after washing it. She said nothing, looking straight ahead as she drove. As the dump came into sight, I felt a hand squeeze my heart real tight and I couldn't breathe right. She pulled the car close to where the trash was, and she left the engine running.

"Let him out," she said.

Ben opened the car door. I was still holding Smokey. I knew he was afraid because he started to shake. He refused to budge, his hind legs trembling as he tried to dig them into the car seat. Ben finally had to get out and pull him out by the skin on his neck, since he had no collar. A bitter taste rose in my throat and I had to keep swallowing so I wouldn't throw up.

Ben finally got Smokey Joe out of the car and climbed back in, slamming the door. Mother took off fast, the car tires throwing up dirt and dust as we sped off. Ben and I watched out the back window as Smokey ran as hard as he could after the car. We were both screaming and crying and telling Mother to stop, but she just drove faster.

For once I didn't get slapped for crying.

When we got home, I hid behind the shed and cried. The sight of Smokey Joe running as hard as he could to catch up to us was a sight I couldn't unsee. I wondered what Ben was doing, but I didn't try to find him because I knew he'd never cry in front of me. Mother never said a word about Smokey from that day on, and neither did I. I could only hope he was able to survive on the scraps from the dump and pray that God would allow him to live.

In spite of her seeming hardheartedness, I loved my mother. She often went hungry so the rest of us could eat. Her life had forced her to be practical rather than sentimental. She had suffered a lot in life, from being raised in a violent family to losing many of the people she loved.

One of the people she lost was my sister. Five years before I was born, my mother had a little girl whom she named Nelda Jane and called "Janie." When Janie was a toddler, she developed a severe cold and fever and began struggling to breathe. Daddy rode into town on horseback in the dead of winter to get the doctor, but by the time they arrived back at the house, Janie had passed. Mother was inconsolable, I was told. No matter where we moved— from Texas to Arkansas to Texas again and finally on to Oregon—Mother carried her picture of Janie, with her blond, curly hair and blue eyes, and hung it on the wall.

The loss of Janie, coupled with the fact that she didn't relish the poverty and hard work that would come with having more children, made Mother reluctant to become pregnant again. However, she mistakenly believed that it would be the only way to keep Daddy out of the war. It was only after she had Ben and me that she heard farmers were exempt from the draft.

Her life became a tedious one of working at whatever job she could find, following Daddy around as he searched for a better life and trying to keep her family from starving.

Ben and I entered the fourth and fifth grades in Eugene, Oregon. I was now known as "Kay," although in a few years, that would change. Once again, I ran into problems at school. The teacher had put me in one of the lower reading groups, which made me feel as if I wasn't as smart as the other kids.

My life immediately improved, however, when my big sister Barbara transferred from the phone company in Amarillo to the one in Eugene. My stomach was doing flip-flops as we drove to the Greyhound bus station to meet her.

"She's here!" I shouted, finding my voice for once. I ran to her for a big hug. I was happy to have my sister and bed partner back again.

Other than feeling like I was stupid in school, I liked living in Oregon. I played with a few of the kids on the street where we lived. None were in my class and I didn't make any other friends at school. That was okay with me, because I had never had school friends. I didn't really think about it because at recess, I always got in line and played tetherball, and friends weren't needed for that.

Daddy had finally given Barbara permission to go out on her first date since she was out of high school and working.

"Where are you going? What are you going to do? What are you going to wear?"

I had a million questions for her, and like any little sister would, I pestered her until she finally told me to shut up and let her figure it out.

I tried to stay awake until she came home, but I fell sound asleep and was only awakened by the sound of her crying in the bathroom. She was washing off some dried blood between her legs, and I noticed bruises were beginning to show on her thighs. A big lump formed in my throat, but I couldn't speak. I wanted to put my arms around her, but she just said, "Get back in bed and I'll be there in a minute," as she continued washing the blood off her inner thigh.

She was shaking and crying when she crawled into bed. I scooted as close to her as I could, hoping I could make her stop crying. She told me the man she had gone out with had done a bad thing to her. The next morning she told me he had forced himself on her, not using the word "rape," but I was still able to understand what she meant.

Not too long after that, Barbara decided to return to

Texas. I moped around the house, not eating, because I was afraid I'd never see her again. I never knew whether she told our parents about the incident or not. At the time she made me promise not to tell them. I knew she felt ashamed because I was certain the blue bruises had floated off her body and surrounded her. I could feel them and see them, but I tried to bury the memory. I wished she could have hit that man so hard he couldn't have hurt her. Then she could have stayed with us.

Daddy and Gerald worked in Oakridge, Oregon, a small logging town. It was decided that we should move there so we could all be together and not just see Daddy and Gerald on weekends.

Oakridge was surrounded by forest and had a sawmill, a few stores, and a movie theater. That was about it. I immediately decided I wanted to see a movie, which cost twenty-five cents, but I knew I would need to babysit or do something to get the money to go to the show.

I started sixth grade and made friends with a neighbor girl, Francie, who lived with her mother and grandmother. She invited me to her house on weekends to watch television. I loved *The Lone Ranger*. When we weren't watching TV, we played tetherball for hours in her back yard. Her grandmother made delicious sandwiches. Francie was my first real friend. I thought she was pretty, so tall and slender, with long, wavy brown hair and a few freckles across her nose.

I was thrilled when Barbara came all the way from Texas to visit us for a week. She was smiling when she walked out the door of the bus station and hugged us all. We only had two bedrooms, so she had to sleep on the couch with me, but that was okay. Her head would be at one end of the couch and mine at the other, and we'd talk until I fell asleep. I pestered her with all kinds of questions about where she lived, what she did, and I made her explain her job to me.

The day before she left, she took Ben and me to see *Twenty Thousand Leagues Under the Sea.* I kept imagining what the movie would be like and after what felt like an eternity, we left the house for the theater. Barbara paid for our tickets, and I was proud she could do this for us. We watched a cartoon and then the movie started. I sat on the edge of my seat, forgetting that it was just a movie. It became my world. When I learned the movie was based on a book by Jules Verne, I checked it out of the school library and read it at least three times.

Twenty Thousand Leagues Under the Sea marked the beginning of my love for reading. Before that, my reading choices had been the Bible and whatever we had to read at school, which must have been plenty boring because I didn't remember any of it.

Since Gerald and Daddy both had steady work, my parents were able to save enough money to buy a small lot. Daddy and Gerald worked all week at the sawmill and on Saturdays, they started building a house on the lot. Mother had drawn a picture of the house she wanted.

At long last, Daddy began making plans to fulfill his dream of going into the ministry. He rented the local Legion Hall to hold services. Ben and I had the job of going to the hall with Daddy early Sunday morning to sweep up the beer bottles and cigarette butts and empty the ashtrays from Saturday night. The whole place still reeked of beer and cigarettes throughout the Sunday service. The old wooden floor had absorbed so much beer it would never smell good again. The big hall was always cold, even in the summer.

Daddy recruited a few men and their families from the mill for the Sunday services. Usually ten to twelve people showed up. Mother played the upright piano, which had cigarette burns all over the top of it. Gerald led the singing and I would sing as loud as I could, even though Mother laughed and said I couldn't carry a tune if I had it in a bucket. Daddy preached a *hell fire and damnation* sermon. Ben and I sat in the very front of the room.

Daddy was a dynamic preacher. He really got into the preaching, using hand gestures, roaming back and forth in front of the pulpit. He couldn't stand in one spot. He often paused as if to give us time to let his words sink in. Daddy was bald, except around the edges of his head, and he had a big Roman nose. I thought people had to listen to him because the way he looked demanded it. I can't remember ever being bored by his preaching. My favorite sermon was from Romans 3:23-24. *For all have sinned and come short of the glory of God. Being justified freely by his grace through the redemption that is in Christ Jesus* (King James version). That was my favorite passage, because there was a way of being redeemed for your sins and still making it into heaven.

Daddy had finally achieved his goal of becoming a minister and providing for his family. We were even building a new house. I had a good friend at last and plenty of food to eat.

There had been rumors that a strike at the mill was brewing. I overheard my parents talking, and Daddy made it clear he did not want any part of it. He just wanted to keep on working. But the strike happened and the mill closed down. Both Daddy and Gerald were out of a job.

Daddy saw all his hard work and dreams vanish. He was no longer able to support the mission he had started, and his dream to eventually have a little church built so we didn't have to hold services at the Legion Hall was dead.

I was eleven years old when Daddy suffered what the doctors called a *nervous breakdown*, now called a clinical depression. He slept most of the day and night. The doctor told Mother she had to take him back to Eugene for treatment. Gerald gave her all the money he had and Mother added it to the last of her money. We moved back to Eugene with no money and no jobs.

Ben, Mother and Kay

We were homeless, but Mother figured out a way to live and earn some money. Hard work wasn't new to her, nor to the rest of us.

It was bean-picking season. We camped out in a tent and picked beans all summer. With the money we earned, we hoped we could find a house to live in when the season was over. Daddy's treatments were delayed until there was some money, but he was able to get off the cot and pick beans. Maybe the fact that he had been a farmer most of his life helped him.

I hated living in that tent. It was boiling hot inside during the day and long into the evening. Mother, Daddy, Ben, and I slept crammed almost on top of each other. We hauled our water in buckets from a nearby farmhouse and cooked over an open fire. Any bathing had to be done with a wet washcloth and a bucket of water. At age twelve I was old enough by then to be embarrassed by living this way.

Gerald was lucky enough to find a job in a sawmill in a nearby town. He brought food to us on the weekends. At the end of the summer Gerald and Mother found an old, rundown one-bedroom house across the river from Eugene in a town called Springfield, and we moved in. Daddy continued to act like a ghost around the house. Either he was sleeping or silent, although I could hear the low murmuring of his and Mother's voices at bedtime.

In the 1950s clinical depression was treated with shock treatments and heavy narcotics. In the 1970s, when I saw actor Jack Nicholson receiving shock treatments in *One Flew Over The Cuckoo's Nest*, I was reminded of Daddy's treatments. When I asked Mother why this was done to Daddy, she said that "shocking his brain with electricity would make him forget why he was depressed and his thought pattern would change."

I lay in bed at night and imagined wires hooked up to his head. I envisioned Daddy's body jerking and twisting when the shock went through him. I was afraid to ask Mother if that was really what happened, so that image stayed in my head as the truth.

I didn't see much difference in Daddy's behavior. He still slept a lot and often he would have panic attacks in the middle of the night, jumping up and opening the window, gasping for air. The only other time I saw him get up was at my mother's urging to go to the hospital for another shock treatment.

For what seemed like a year, he never said a word to me. Even before his "nervous breakdown," he had rarely held any kind of a conversation with me. Between work, the mission and building a house, he mostly spent time in his chair, reading the Bible.

In our small house the bathroom was off his bedroom and we had to walk by his bed to use it. He was always asleep. Sometimes I stopped and whispered, "Daddy," but he never opened his eyes. It felt as if the sun no longer shone on our dark little house.

Survival was on Mother's mind. We lived outside the city limits so Mother could keep a cow and chickens. She sold milk and eggs and she planted a garden. She taught me how to make butter using the cream at the top of the gallon jugs. I spooned the cream off the top and put it into a quart jar, put the lid on tight, and shook the jar until the cream turned into little butterballs. I'd spoon it out, leaving the whey, put it on a saucer, and shape it into a ball.

Weeds were waist high in our front yard, so Mother got a goat and staked her out in front of the house to eat the weeds. This caused me no end of embarrassment, so I never had any schoolmates come to my house. Instead, I walked into town if I wanted to see my one friend. I asked Mother why we didn't get a lawn mower like everyone else. She pointed to the goat and said in her matter-of-fact way, "We have one."

Gerald, Ben and I all slept in the "front room." There was a double bed for Ben and Gerald and a cot for me. We had no closets, so I threw my clothes in a cardboard box and slid it under the bed.

I had given a lot of thought to how to avoid having any friends come to my house, but the best-laid plans don't always work. One Saturday during the summer, Mother had to go into town so she told me to milk the cow. I had trouble with that cow. I knew how to milk her; it was getting her to stand still that was the problem. She seemed to know when a less experienced person was milking her.

Like a fool I went out to do the chore barefoot. I put the rope around her head and tied it to the fence post. I sat down on the stool, but she kept sidestepping back and forth as I tried to milk her. I had no patience left and slapped her on the rump, causing her to kick the milk bucket over, spilling what little milk I had managed to get. Now I knew I was in trouble. Not only did we need the milk, but a cow has to be relieved of her milk or her udder becomes hard and sore. I had to try again.

I had about a half bucket of milk when I heard someone call out, "Kay!"

I looked up and saw a boy from church smiling at me. I jumped up and stepped back into a cow pie. I looked down in horror as it oozed up between my toes. As I was staring at my feet, the cow sidestepped and landed on my foot with her back leg. I slapped her on the side and she moved. My foot felt like it was broken, but I couldn't howl in pain because that might have caused the boy to want to stay and help.

"Do you want to go for a walk?" he asked.

I was embarrassed and wanted to get rid of him as quickly as possible. "No," I replied, "I have to get cleaned up and go somewhere."

He left, looking rather dejected. The next Sunday I refused to go to church because I didn't want to see him. After that, I never talked to him in church. I didn't want him to feel he had to talk to me. After seeing where I lived, I figured he didn't want to, anyway.

Mother told me a few days later that I had to milk the cow. I didn't often defy her, but I thought I was old enough to say no.

"Mother, I will not milk that cow again. She hates me. Besides, dirt gets in the bucket when she kicks it over, and we could all die of disease from the dirt in the milk... *and* she almost broke my foot. You don't want to have to take me to the doctor, do you, if she does it again?"

Mother stared straight into my eyes and calmly told me that I didn't have to milk the cow anymore. Relief flooded over me. Before I reached the house, though, Mother said, "Now, go milk the goat!"

I knew I had lost my battle. I got the milk bucket for Betsy the goat and went to the front yard to get her. Not wanting the neighbors to witness my humiliation, I took her around to the back of the house.

Goats have one big udder with two small teats. I could hardly squeeze out the milk because the teats are short. About forty-five minutes later, after much effort, I finally finished milking her. It had taken me twice as long as it would have taken to milk the cow. As Betsy turned her head and looked at me, I sensed her relief that I was done. I'm sure she was as frustrated as I was with the milking.

I learned it just wasn't worth it to defy Mother.

At the end of the summer, Mother said I could buy some material to make myself some school clothes. She taught me how to make skirts and helped me with the blouses. For the first time I felt as if I was dressed as well as most of the other kids. I was thankful we had enough to eat, and I was glad that I seemed to fit in at school. I could even tolerate the goat in the front yard, although my fervent wish was that none of my schoolmates ever had the opportunity to see where I lived.

Most of the girls in my physical education class had already started wearing bras. As I stared at my chest in the bathroom mirror at home, I thought that my breasts were about the size of walnuts, not nice, round tomatoes like the other girls' breasts. I was a typical teenager, worrying that I didn't have boobs. The workers in the bean fields had called me "String Bean Katy" because I looked like a bean pole with two little bumps.

At the end of gym class, I tried to pretend I was invisible as I walked into the big, open shower with shower heads spaced a few feet apart. I wanted to hide, but there was no way to get out of showering, especially since the teacher stood and barked our names out as we entered the shower. I didn't look at the other girls, who continued talking to each other as if they weren't even naked. The thought of five more years of dressing with my back to everyone, covering my chest with my shirt, and fumbling with my clothes to get them back on as soon as possible threw me into complete agony. I could only hope that some day I would have breasts the size of tomatoes, too.

~~~~~~~~

We were all excited when relatives from Texas came to visit us in Oregon. We lived so far away that it was rare for anyone to make such a long trip to the northwest. The adults got caught up on all the family gossip while Ben and I had fun playing with the four children, who were close to our ages. We didn't even mind when Mother told us we'd need to give up our bed and sleep on pallets on the floor under the kitchen table.

The weekend before the family planned to leave, Mother said we could have a picnic in the park. I hadn't been on a picnic before, but I was really excited about it. In my mind I pictured a table in the woods, covered with food. All us kids would be running around and playing in the nearby river with the sun shining on us. We packed food and everyone climbed into the car.

We drove for about thirty minutes and finally saw the sign pointing to the picnic grounds. There were tables under tall trees and, of course, the river was nearby. We ran straight for the river, where we splashed and waded and tried to walk on top of a fish barrier without falling off.

I was getting hungry and went back to the picnic area. My relative's husband told me it was time to eat and asked me to show him where the rest of the kids were. We headed back into the woods in the direction of the river.

Just before we got there, he reached down and pulled up my shirt. "Let me have a little nibble," he said. He loomed over me and I saw his face and mouth coming toward my chest. Terrified, I turned and began running. I could feel the paintbrush painting this picture in my head.

"Don't tell your daddy or he'll kill me," he yelled as I ran back to where the car was parked.

I crawled into the back seat of the car, hanging my head out the door to throw up. I could only throw up spit, though, because I had an empty stomach. I lay there and listened to the flies buzzing and felt the warmth of the sun as the bile rose in my throat. To keep from vomiting again, I pretended I was floating around in the clouds. I finally fell asleep, missing the chance to eat.

No one asked me why I had lain in the car, not eating.

When we got home, my relative's husband told me he would buy me a bicycle. I said I didn't want one, although in my heart I really did. Just not from him. I felt shame and couldn't bring myself to tell Mother. I thought somehow it must have been my fault and I would be blamed. I knew I had to keep this secret hidden, just as I had kept the secret of Barbara's rape.

I didn't like crawling under the table to sleep with the other kids anymore. I wanted to curl up somewhere by myself and sleep forever. Thankfully, our relatives left the next day. I didn't go outside to wave goodbye. When I heard the car backing out, I could breathe again. I wondered if what I'd experienced happened to all girls when they got breasts.

Maybe when I could buy a bra, it would serve as protection. I sure hoped so.

~~~~~~~~

In spite of what had happened over the summer, I was feeling pretty good about things as I started the eighth grade in a newly built school. It was my second year with the same kids and I was now part of "the group." I had made a good friend and finally had someone to do things with on a regular basis. We never went to each other's houses, though, and I wondered if hers might be as bad as mine.

I decided I wanted to have the same things as the other kids, like nice clothes and money to buy candy from the machines at school. I knew my parents couldn't give me anything—Mother was working in a laundry pressing pants on a big steaming machine and Daddy wasn't working—so I was determined to get a job. A neighbor named Donna asked me to babysit her two-year-old son and I immediately said, "Sure." I didn't know a thing about small children, but I didn't tell her that. She had agreed to make me a new dress as payment.

The little boy had already eaten dinner by the time I

arrived. All I had to do was give him dessert around eight, get him into his pajamas, and put him to bed. I was excited about being able to watch TV after he went to bed because our family didn't own a TV.

We both savored the red Jell-O his mom had left for us, and when he said he couldn't sleep, I lay down beside him and told him a story. The next thing I knew, his mother was shaking me.

"Wake up, Kay!"

I figured Donna would never ask me to babysit again. I had fallen asleep with the light on and she probably thought I was irresponsible. I was relieved when she continued to ask me to babysit, even if the jobs didn't come often.

I needed another job if I was going to buy more school clothes and lunches. Mother told me about a man who needed to have his house cleaned once a week and was willing to pay five dollars. He worked in a sawmill, along with his two grown sons, who also lived in the house. I took the job, even though I knew little about housekeeping other than washing dishes, making beds, and sweeping floors.

On my first day of work, I couldn't believe my eyes. It was worse than any house I had ever lived in. The sink was filled with dirty dishes and green fuzz was growing in the bottom of the cups. The countertop was filthy and all throughout the house, ashtrays were overflowing with cigarette butts. Piles of dirty clothes were strewn about. I began by washing the dishes and putting them in the rack to drain while I wiped down the countertops. This was harder than I thought it would be because dried food was stuck all over every surface. Sometimes I had to pry the food off with a knife. I gathered up all the ashtrays, emptied them, washed them, and stacked them on the counter. I dusted, swept out the kitchen and living room, and moved on to the bedrooms, where I was in for another shock.

Kay at Age 13

The sheets on the unmade beds were filthy. Upon closer inspection I could see lipstick smears on the sheets, black bobby pins here and there, and ugly yellow stains. I was still a kid, but it was obvious to me what had happened in those rooms.

Fortunately, there was a washing machine. After I put all the sheets in the machine, however, I realized I didn't have any idea how to start it. At home we had a wringer washer that plugged in to start it up. I had to make this thing work somehow. I began punching buttons and water started pouring into the tub. I crammed the dirty sheets down and closed the lid. I hadn't seen any soap so I let them wash without it. I figured they would come out cleaner than when they went in. Later I hung them on the clothesline to dry.

By that time, it was getting dark and I knew I had to start walking home, even if I wasn't finished. I picked up the five-dollar bill I had been eyeing every time I passed by it. Boy, did I feel I had earned it.

I wondered if the guy would fire me since I hadn't

gotten everything done. He didn't, though, so once a week after school I trudged over to his house and cleaned his filthy rooms all over again.

Each time there was a five-dollar bill waiting for me. I felt rich.

I wasn't a good student, but I still managed to pass every class. I even passed algebra, which didn't make a lick of sense to me, and of course I had no one who could help me. I felt lucky to have a passing grade of "D" at the end of the year. Neither Mother nor Daddy ever looked at any of my report cards, so I simply signed Mother's name and returned them.

I could see that Mother was overwhelmed by her life. Since Daddy was still having shock treatments off and on and mostly slept all day, everything fell upon Mother. Her job at a laundry, pressing pants on a big steam machine that she operated with a foot pedal, was exhausting. She had to place the leg of the pants on the machine and hit the foot pedal to close the top down on the pant leg. The hot steam caused sweat to roll off her face. By the time she got home, she could barely get dinner on the table, and when she couldn't, my brother and I would eat whatever we could find. Sometimes there was cold boiled cabbage and maybe cold cornbread. It tasted good, though, because we were always hungry.

My big brother Gerald was still working and contributing to the family. Ben had gotten a job working in a mechanic shop after school, so he had money to buy his clothes and gas for his old car. In spite of Daddy not having a job, we did have income.

Things suddenly changed when Gerald was drafted into the Army.

We lost his monetary support, but more importantly for me, I lost my biggest supporter. He seemed to be the only one who cared about me. Every now and then, he had given me a dollar. He knew I was crazy about Elvis Presley, so he bought me a little record player for Christmas. Later, he was sorry he had done it, though, because I played the few "45s" I owned over and over again. Gerald came home from work one day and announced, "If I have to hear Elvis one more time, I'm throwing you and that record player out the door!" He dragged out the name "El-vis," enunciating both syllables. I knew he didn't mean it. Gerald could never do anything mean or hurt anyone's feelings.

After he left for the Army, Mother got a job working nights at the Juvenile Hall in Springfield, Oregon. Daddy was pretty much in bed all the time. Ben, who was now in high school, was starting to do what high school boys do—drink and carouse around. I did some things with Ben's friends, like driving around, looking for something to do. One morning Mother came home with Ben in tow at six in the morning. Seemed he and some buddies were caught drinking beer and were all hauled into Juvenile Hall.

That same night I had been driving my friend's car and got pulled over for speeding on Main Street. I didn't even have a permit to drive. The cop didn't give me a ticket, but he did give me a stern lecture.

I asked Mother what she was doing with Ben. "He spent the night with me at the hall," she said, "and I'm lucky you didn't, too!" Evidently the cop who hauled Ben in to Juvenile Hall was the same one who had lectured me about speeding. Then he had ratted me out to my mother. *What a jerk*, I thought. *He didn't have to do that.*

Ben's hearing was scheduled for the following Friday, and that night, he got caught drinking beer again. This time, when he arrived at "Juvy," Mother was fired. Her boss had told her she couldn't work there any more if she couldn't even handle her own kids.

During the time Mother worked at the Juvenile Hall, managing the girls who were there, no one was "managing" Ben and me. I could have stayed out all night and she never would have known. But she did know some things.

I was seeing a boy who worked at a gas station in town, and he usually parked his car down the road, waiting for Mother to leave for work around eight o'clock. Then we would go to the drive-in for a hamburger. Like many teenagers I knew from school, we did little more than kiss and "pet" on our dates. I wanted to be like the other kids, whose parents set rules, so I told him I had to be home by midnight.

It wasn't until much later that I learned Mother had seen the boy's car parked and waiting every Friday and Saturday night as she left for work. She had worried about me, but she never talked to me about it. I never knew that she knew about my dates, and she never knew that I gave myself a "curfew" in an effort to fit in with the other kids and stay out of trouble.

I had no idea trouble would soon find me anyway.

6 TEXAS AND BACK AGAIN

Summer came and I didn't look forward to cleaning houses, babysitting, or picking beans. An opportunity came from my sister. She needed me to come to Lubbock, Texas, for the summer and babysit her one-year-old child, Paula.

Barbara was three months' pregnant with her second child and had returned to work at the telephone company. Her husband Harold drove trucks part time and attended school part time. I didn't like Harold at all. He always told me how to take care of Paula, but I felt that his bossiness did not come from any real concern about Paula. Instead, I thought he constantly wanted to prove to me that he could tell me what to do and I had to obey.

My morning routine involved fixing a bottle for Paula when she woke up about six o'clock, waiting for her to go back to sleep, and then returning to bed myself. One morning, after I had gone back to bed, I suddenly felt someone getting into my bed. I opened my eyes and was shocked to see Harold next to me. I could tell by the look on his face that he was planning to do something bad to me. He had a goofy looking half-smile on his face and wasn't saying anything. I was on the side of the bed that was against the wall, but I knew I had to get out of there. As I tried to scramble down to the foot of the bed to escape, he grabbed me, putting his hand over my mouth and pulling down the bottom of my pajamas with the other hand. He was lying halfway on top of me as he raped me. I felt as if I was suffocating and his weight was crushing me. I had flashes of my sister being me as he brutally rammed himself inside me. I thought he was tearing my insides out down there. He still had his hand over my mouth and I could hardly breathe. I could see the enlarged cords in his neck as he strained. The paintbrush was painting another image in my mind that would never go away. I heard a roaring sound like the air was being sucked out of the room. I gasped for breath and he finally got off me.

I stumbled to the bathroom with blood between my legs. I was crying. He opened the bathroom door and slouched against the door frame, watching me as I tried to wipe the blood away.

"I didn't think you were a virgin or I wouldn't have bothered you," he said casually.

I felt the most hatred in my heart that I had ever felt for anyone. I grabbed a bar of soap off the sink and threw it at him. By continuing to stare at me, he made me feel as if he was raping me all over again. I pulled my pajama bottoms up and felt a hot flush as he gazed at me. He didn't move, so I had to push my way past him. He followed me out the door, threatening to kick me out of the house if I told Barbara.

I didn't know what to do. I felt trapped. On the few days Harold was home on the weekends, Barbara could tell that I hated him but she didn't know why. I finally asked her to give me the money to take the bus back to Oregon. Barbara still needed a babysitter, but Harold told her to give me the money. He wanted me out of there. The longer I stayed, the more he feared I would tell what he had done.

I knew I had another secret I had to keep deep within

me. I didn't want my sister to be hurt, so I couldn't tell her. Harold was mean enough to her as it was, and she had a child, with another on the way. Who else could I tell? No one.

I took the Greyhound bus back to Oregon and started my sophomore year in high school. I had begun to feel like the other girls last year, fitting in at last, but no more. Because of the rape, I felt worthless and out of place. I couldn't tell anyone what Harold had done, so I pushed it into the back of my mind and tried to forget about it.

There were more enrollment papers to be filled out. I decided to enroll under the name of Kathy, the name my mother had always wanted me to use. I felt I was no longer the person that I had been and my new name would prove it to me.

Mother signed the enrollment papers after she made sure I hadn't written anything down about Daddy having a nervous breakdown. She had ingrained that in us. No one was to know. I thought nobody had a family like mine and was ashamed of my father and his illness.

I had thought about college in the past, but now any idea about talking to Mother about it disappeared from my mind. I stopped seeing my friend or participating in any activities. My grades were lousy, but I didn't care. I felt as if I was just going through the motions of living.

"Hi, I'm Tom. Do you want to go out sometime?"

I was startled one day by this sudden introduction of a boy in my history class. I had noticed him before. For one thing, he was very good looking, and for another, he was a senior taking a sophomore class for some reason. We all suspected it was because he had either failed the class or missed taking it when he was a sophomore or junior. I didn't care. I was just flattered to be noticed by him and to be asked out on a date.

"Yes," I stammered, and he said he'd see me in the next class.

After the next class he said, "If I can get my brother's car, I'll pick you up Friday night, okay?"

The first thought I had was *Oh, no, then he'll see where I live*, but I put that out of my mind and agreed. I was so flustered that I didn't think to ask what time or where we were going.

Friday night I agonized, wondering when he would pick me up. Except for Daddy, who was sleeping, I was alone. He finally arrived around seven o'clock, coming down our dirt driveway, filled with potholes, in an old, dented car. I noticed that the door on the driver's side was a different color from the rest of the car. He said we had to stop by his house and pick up something, but I didn't have the sense to ask him what he was picking up or where we were going. I felt tongue-tied, not knowing how to make conversation.

Soon we arrived at a rundown house that was worse than mine. Tom disappeared inside for a minute before he came back out the front door, carrying a paper sack.

"We make home brew," he said. "We can drink this."

He pulled out two bottles of beer. I had never tasted beer, but I figured I'd give it a try. Tom drove to Blueberry Hill, which by reputation was where high schoolers went to make out. When I took a drink of the beer, I was glad it was too dark for him to see the face I made. This was the worst stuff I had ever tasted. He was happily drinking his beer, and when he noticed I had stopped drinking mine, he took it and finished it off. We started making out.

I worried about whether or not I was kissing the right way. Should I do anything besides kiss? Suddenly there was a knock on the fogged-up driver's side window. We hastily adjusted ourselves as Tom rolled down the window and looked up at the cop standing there.

"What are you doing, sonny, looking for Sputnik?" the cop asked sarcastically.

Tom stammered that we were just talking.

"Well, go somewhere else to talk," the cop replied.

"You don't need to be sitting in a car up here, freezing your tails off."

That was the end of our first date.

We talked a little as we drove back to my house. Tom explained that he missed classes because he needed to work, driving a tractor in the bean fields to make some money. The following Monday I didn't see him in class, but I continued to see him whenever he could scrounge up a car. We never did anything but drink beer (and he usually drank mine) and look for a place to park and make out. I knew he didn't have money to take me to the movies or do anything else. Maybe he was ashamed to take me to his house, because I never went inside.

He graduated at the end of the school year and immediately joined the Navy. I didn't know if I would ever see him again.

Tom wasn't the only one who left that summer. My brother Ben, who had been such an important part of my life since the days we got into mischief in Texas, had graduated and joined the Air Force.

My brother Gerald was still away, serving in the Army. Daddy hadn't recovered and continued to sleep away his days, while my only friend had moved to another high school.

Mother kept putting one foot in front of the other, working at whatever job she could find. I continued to feel different from the other girls at school and I thought they sensed it, so I didn't try to make any friends. My clothes weren't as nice as theirs and I knew I could never invite them to my house. I was lonely and wondered how long I could go on existing like this.

I refused to get out of bed and go to church any more. Why should I? God wasn't going to help me. That was clear.

My decision prompted Daddy to actually get out of bed.

"You are going to burn in the pits of Hell!" he yelled at

me one Sunday morning when I wouldn't dress for church. His face was contorted and angry. It was unusual for Daddy to display a temper. "Well, now, Mary," he had always said mildly to Mother when she got angry. And when Ben and I got out of control, he would only yell a little bit. This was different. I covered my head in order to stop seeing him. I am already in a version of Hell, I thought to myself.

Daddy finally gave up on me and left the room. Even he recognized that I was hopeless.

~~~~~~~~~

I hadn't been sure if I would ever see Tom again, but I came back to life when he suddenly came home on leave from the Navy. We saw each other the entire time, and I felt good about having a boyfriend. We were sitting on the couch at his sister's house one day when he shocked me by saying, "Maybe we should get married before I go back to San Diego."

A million thoughts went through my head. I had no idea why he wanted to get married. His proposal certainly wasn't romantic in any way. What would I do about school? I didn't want to drop out. What about Mother? Would she say it was okay? I listened as Tom explained the practical reasons for our marriage. He was stationed on a destroyer and would be going out to sea often. He could find an apartment for us before I came to San Diego. He said I would be able to get something called an "allotment" every month that would help pay the rent.

It was an opportunity to start over, I realized. To escape. I would be able to get out of Eugene, Oregon, and the house I was ashamed of with the father inside who slept all the time and the mother who did nothing but work and never had time to talk to me. And I did have a crush on Tom. Maybe it was love. How would I know that?

"Yes," I stammered to Tom. The word caught in my throat but finally came out. I was going to get married.

The next day I told Daddy the news. He had gotten out

of bed and was sitting in a chair in the living room.

"You ain't gonna amount to a hill of beans," he said.

I couldn't reply. I was shocked that Daddy would say such a thing to me. He hadn't talked to me for over a year, other than to yell at me to go to church, so how could he know me or what I was going to amount to? I walked out of the room, feeling devastated.

I was sixteen and Tom was eighteen when we got married. My parents didn't object and gave their permission since I was under age. Mother told me later that she suspected I was pregnant, which I wasn't. Tom and I still hadn't had sex.

Mother arranged for us to marry in the church she and Daddy attended. The only other people there were Tom's mother and sister. After the ceremony Mother told me she saw my legs visibly shaking.

Our honeymoon night was spent at Tom's sister's house. It was freezing cold, so we went to bed early to get warm. I was scared Tom would discover I wasn't a virgin. If he did, he never said so. I really didn't think he had the experience to know.

Tom had to leave the next day so I tried to get close to him in the bed. I just wanted him to hold me and say nice things to me. But every time I moved closer, he mistakenly thought I wanted to have sex again, so it turned out to be a very sleepless night for me. I stared at the ceiling, wondering if things were supposed to be different. I wished I had been able to talk to Mother about everything.

Tom's sister took me home the next day after she took Tom to the airport. I crawled into my bed and cried quietly so Daddy couldn't hear me. What had I gotten myself into? I was still stuck at home. I hadn't escaped. When I went to school the next morning, I told no one about my marriage. Who would I tell?

Little did I know that I had jumped out of the frying pan into the fire.

7 SAN DIEGO

S hortly after marrying Tom, I discovered that technically, I didn't exist. Kay-Doll, Kay, Kathy... none of those girls had ever been born in the eyes of the government.

I didn't have a birth certificate.

I had applied to the United States Navy for my allotment of $91.30 per month so I could join Tom in San Diego. The Navy required that I supply my birth certificate; however, our family doctor, Dr. Butts, had failed to file the document after I was born. (He had also listed incorrect names for both of my brothers on their birth certificates.) Mother, always too busy, had forgotten about it.

Usually a person in my situation could take the family Bible to the courthouse and show the clerk the name and birthdate recorded in the Bible. However, we didn't live in the Red River Valley where I was born, so from our home in Oregon, Mother and I began the arduous process of obtaining a birth certificate. She wrote to the courthouse in Red River County and was informed by return letter that an affidavit was needed from a non-relative who had witnessed my birth. There was no such person.

A friend from church then told Mother that if I had ever

been listed on a U.S. Census, I could use that as proof that I was born. Mother told me that she remembered a census had been taken when we lived in Arkansas. She wrote to the county seat and they sent the document, showing that I was six years old at the time the census was taken. I guessed that this was finally my payoff for living in Arkansas.

I filled out the papers and mailed them back to Texas. When I asked my mother how my middle name of Kathryn was spelled, she replied, "You can spell it any way you want to." (I chose Kathryn, but later learned from my sister that when Mother put our names in her Bible, she had spelled it Katherine.)

The certificate finally arrived in the mail. I took it out and the first thing I saw were the words in capital letters across the top of the page: DELAYED BIRTH CERTIFICATE. I felt different when I looked at it. I somehow had the feeling that nothing was normal with me, not even the proof of my birth. I was also worried the U.S. Navy wouldn't accept such a document.

It took until May of 1960 to get the documents from the U.S. Navy, affirming that I was eligible for an allotment. It took until school was out in June to get the first government check.

I had finished my junior year. Mother and I talked about my leaving, and she said I could put my clothes in a cardboard box and tie it up real well with twine. She took me to the Greyhound bus station to purchase a ticket and leave for San Diego. Tom had been looking for a place for us to live and had found a studio apartment. He was getting thirty-one dollars every two weeks. All we had to live on each month was one hundred fifty-three dollars.

When we got to the bus station, Mother gave me a hug. That was the only hug I could ever remember from her. All the way to the station, I had wondered if she'd hug me, and I was surprised when she did.

I remembered that hug and how good it made me feel all the way to San Diego.

The studio apartment was furnished, but it was really awful. It had cockroaches, one of the insects I hated and feared most. I often dreamed of them crawling down the wall and into the bed. I'd wake up in a sweat and turn on the light to check the bed, and they would scatter across the floor.

Tom was home for two weeks before he shipped out for the next few months. My nightmares got worse and I spent half the night worrying, wondering what I should do next. I knew I had to finish high school, so that would be my first priority.

I didn't know anyone, so I started exploring on my own, walking around the streets near the apartment, locating the grocery store and buying food. I didn't know how to cook anything and I didn't have a cookbook, so I stuck to things like canned soup, eggs and bologna sandwiches.

San Diego had beautiful, warm weather, and it was nice to just walk around and see all the houses and apartments. Boy, was it different from rainy old Oregon. This was the biggest town I had ever lived in.

I saw signs for the San Diego Zoo. I had never been to a zoo and had no idea how to get there. One day, as I was coming back to the apartment, a lady was unlocking her door a few doors down from mine. I screwed up my courage and asked her how I could take the bus to the zoo. She invited me in and showed me a bus schedule. I had learned the names of the streets just by walking around, so I understood when she told me to go to a particular street and wait for the bus with a certain number on it. Or, she said, it may even say "San Diego Zoo" on the front of the bus.

The next morning I set out for the zoo. I was really excited but not sure what to expect. I boarded the bus and after a few minutes, I got scared when I saw people pull a cord to have the bus stop so they could get off. I didn't know when to pull the cord. I was frozen in my seat, but after a few stops and only a few people left on the bus, the driver stopped and announced that we were at the zoo. Relief flooded through me. I got off, along with several other people, and followed them to the entrance. When I paid the entrance fee, I was provided with a map. That's when I learned that I didn't know how to read a map.

I sat down on a bench and started figuring it out. The lions, tigers, giraffes, elephants and monkeys were on the top of my list. I found my way to each of the enclosures, but along the way I saw exotic birds, penguins and signs for a snake house. I decided I would stick to the big animals first. As I viewed the lions and tigers, I saw that they all paced back and forth in their small cages. They repeated the same behavior over and over. When I saw the elephants, they were doing the same thing, and I became aware they were suffering. They were caged with no escape. I wondered what went through their minds with all the people staring and calling to them.

I decided it was time for me to leave, because their situation was beginning to make me sad. I found my way back to the bus stop and boarded the bus. As I walked to my apartment, I felt just like I imagined the lions and tigers felt. I knew my future wasn't going to be very good. My cage was small, with no escape.

Every six months Tom had to go overseas on the destroyer USS *Ingersoll*. He sent me thirty dollars a month, and I also had my allotment of ninety-one dollars. I don't know how I survived on this, but I know that I ate only enough food to keep myself alive. I realized I had been pretty stupid to get married. I hadn't escaped being hungry like I thought I would.

It was August, and now I had to find a high school and enroll for my senior year. First, though, I had to figure out where I was going and which bus to take. Fortunately, I caught the right bus.

My hands were sweaty and I was scared when I thought about going to a new school. The school seemed enormous, but a sudden feeling of confidence surged through me as I walked into the room marked "Office."

A woman behind the counter looked at me and asked, "Can I help you?"

"Yes, I want to enroll for my senior year."

After a few basic questions, she asked why I wanted to enroll in this school. I explained that I was married and my husband was stationed in San Diego. The look on her face suddenly changed from helpful to closed, as she said, "I'm sorry, but you can't go to school here."

My mouth suddenly went dry. I was afraid and confused and couldn't even seem to ask why I couldn't enroll. The woman went on to explain that because I was married, I had to go to an "alternative continuation school."

"How do I get there?" I stammered.

She wrote down the bus number and I left, still stunned and unable to think clearly.

I had never heard of an alternative continuation school, but I soon learned what it was. I found myself attending E.R. Snyder Continuation High School with kids who had been kicked out of regular high school. The girls were tough and often pregnant. Some carried knives and fought each other. I was afraid to go to the bathroom because of the many fights between the girls. They chose the bathroom because the teachers were less likely to be aware of the fights if they couldn't see them.

One day after class I needed to use the bathroom. I thought I would take my chances since I didn't want to pee my pants. I pushed open the door and saw two girls standing, facing each other, about four feet apart. Both had knives with blades sticking out. The name calling and cursing swirled around the room like thick smoke. I slowly backed out and slunk over to my next class, wondering if I was going to be able to "hold it."

The only good thing about that school was that I could take only the courses I needed, do my work at my own pace, and move on to the next course. I worked at breakneck speed to get out of there. I did fall back on the ill advisement of secretarial training (which I had received in Oregon), even though I knew I wouldn't like it. I took typing and other useful courses to be able to say I was "trained" when I started looking for a job.

Most of the teachers were nice, even the journalism teacher who humiliated me one day.

I was ready to turn in my final assignments and get the last test I needed to take for her class. As I approached her desk, she asked me what I wanted.

"I'm fixing to take the test," I said.

"You're doing *what?*" She asked me this question three times, and each time I felt more and more embarrassed. I didn't know why she kept asking me the same question. The other kids were starting to stare at me. Finally, she reached into the wire basket, picked up the test, and offered it to me, saying "You mean, you are *ready to take* the test."

As I walked slowly back to my desk, holding the test, I thought, *Yes, I am ready to take the test and I am fixing to take it*. This was one of the first times I became aware that I said things differently. I needed to fix this problem.

I finished that test and all the others and was glad to get out of that school. I just wanted to find a job and buy a car. I was confident that the skills I'd developed would land me a decent job.

Now that I was no longer in school, I went back to the name "Kay." I felt I had reached a milestone and needed to mark it in my mind. I was no longer consciously thinking about the rape, and I thought I was finally going back to being the "me" that I had been before. I wanted to make a new beginning and forget the painful "Kathy" years.

I paid twenty cents for a local paper advertising "Jobs Available." There was an opening for a secretary at a company called Trane Air Conditioning. I didn't have a resume. Actually, I didn't even know what a resume was or that I needed one. Instead, I went to a pay phone and called the number. A man answered and I asked if I could come in for an interview. When he said yes, I practically jumped for joy. I raced back to the apartment, combed my hair, put on a skirt and blouse, and checked the bus schedule.

Forty-five minutes later I had arrived in the Hillcrest area of San Diego, so nervous I could hardly think. My hands were sweating. It quickly became clear to me that I didn't know a thing about how to interview for a job. I remembered something my brother Gerald always told me when I thought I couldn't do something: "Just buck up and do it!"

I walked slowly through the open door of the office, trying to breathe normally. A short little man was behind a large desk. My eyes took in the rest of the office. On the opposite side of his desk, there was a file cabinet, a much smaller desk, and a wooden desk chair. A typewriter sat on top of the small desk. I felt uncomfortable for some reason, but the man motioned for me to sit in the chair at the small desk.

I sat down and introduced myself. "My name is Kay and I am the one who called about the interview for a secretary job."

He said his name was Mr. Swartz, but his next question convinced me that I wasn't going to get the job.

"Have you worked before?"

I thought about all the jobs I had done in the first sixteen years of my life: picking cotton, babysitting, cleaning houses, picking beans. But then it occurred to me that he was asking if I had been a secretary before. I knew I was doomed. "No," I answered.

He asked me why I thought I was qualified. Gratitude flooded my brain when I realized I could tell him about the courses I had taken in school. I told him I could type, use a ten-key adding machine, and file—and that I was a hard worker.

He told me the job paid thirty-five dollars a week. Wow, I thought, that's a lot of money. I hoped he didn't notice when I crossed my fingers.

He told me I could start the following Monday. I walked out thinking I was the luckiest girl in the whole world. I couldn't wait until Monday.

I had no idea that I would turn out to be such a bad secretary. I didn't even realize how bad I was. I couldn't spell well, and I had a hard time knowing when to start a new paragraph when I listened to his recorded letters. Mr. Swartz wasn't friendly at all, and if I dared to ask a question, he gave a curt answer and looked disgusted. He usually followed that up by walking out of the office, probably thinking what a dummy he had hired.

It was a one-girl office, and I had to type letters, answer the phone, and do anything else he needed me to do. The office was located in a nice old Victorian house in the Hillcrest area of San Diego. There were several other offices in the building, and I made friends with the men who worked there. They didn't have secretaries and there were no other women upstairs where I worked. The men seemed to really like me, although they teased me about my accent. Sometimes when talking to the main office in Los Angeles, I was asked to repeat things I said. I wondered why, because I was speaking clearly. I had the catalogs with all the equipment and the price lists, so I knew the answers to the questions I was being asked.

Finally, I mustered the courage to ask why I was being asked to repeat myself. The man I was talking to told me that he just liked how I talked with my Texas accent. I was relieved that I hadn't been doing anything wrong.

I was stunned when I was suddenly fired. I was also somewhat relieved, because Mr. Swartz was strange and not very nice to me. One time I came in to work and found him asleep under the desk with his legs sticking out. I wondered if his wife had kicked him out. He wasn't even friendly with the other guys in the building. After he fired me, I walked down the stairs with tears in my eyes and almost knocked a man down as he was walking upstairs. He worked down the hall and he asked me what was wrong. I told him what had happened. I felt like a failure and didn't know what I was going to do next. He told me he would try to help me find another job and asked for a way to get in touch with me. I gave him my address because we didn't have a telephone. I doubted he was really going to help me. He probably just felt sorry for me because I looked so pathetic.

The next week, however, I was hired by one of the men who worked in the same building. Jack Tuttle was an electrical engineer in charge of a branch office of Cutler-Hammer, Inc., a company that sold equipment to the military and other agencies. I soon learned about "toggle switches" and switchboards. My salary was thirty-five dollars a week.

I was happy to have a job, but I *really knew* by then that I was a poor speller. I spelled words the way I pronounced them, usually screwing up the vowels. I couldn't blame it on the boss if I got fired again. Instead, one morning Mr. Tuttle walked into the office and tossed a dictionary on my desk.

"Use this," he said.

My problem was that I didn't know when I spelled a word incorrectly, so the dictionary didn't completely resolve the issue. I agonized over the situation and knew I had to make this job work. I bought a cheap little tape recorder and practiced talking like a Californian so I wouldn't be asked to repeat things. I spelled words into the recorder and listened back to the correct spelling so that I could learn it.

Many times Jack dictated letters using words I'd never

heard of, so I would have to ask the man next door to listen to the tape and tell me what the word was. I was trying my best to become a good secretary.

I turned eighteen. The guys in the office liked taking me to lunch and they would buy me a martini, which was the drink of the day. I didn't know how to refuse. The food was good and I did feel grown up at these lunches. I watched how the men held their knives and forks and tried to do the same.

Unfortunately, after returning from the office, I usually fell asleep from the alcohol. When the boss called, the phone rang and rang until the switchboard picked up. Each time panic set in when I woke up and realized I had fallen asleep. I would slink down to the switchboard and pick up messages from the operator. Invariably, there was a message from my boss, Jack.

The men from the other offices told me that Jack had asked them if he should fire me. They all said no.

I eventually learned how to spell a little better and how to properly set up a letter. I stopped worrying so much about getting fired and settled into my job.

I had been able to exert some control over my work life by educating myself and working hard. That didn't necessarily work for my home life, though, as I discovered.

8 MOTHERHOOD

We bought a car! When Tom came home from one of his out-to-sea trips, we went car shopping. I had managed to save most of my paychecks, so we bought a 1956 Ford Crown Victoria. It was 1962, so the car was six years old and a "rattletrap." It was all we could afford, but I was very proud to own it.

Tom kept telling me that he wanted a son. By that time I had a clue I was probably in a bad marriage and that I should do everything possible to keep from getting pregnant. Tom's drinking was becoming a problem. He was never home, and when he was, he never discussed anything with me. He led his life and I led mine, such as it was.

The only birth control I knew about was a diaphragm. Tom refused to wear a condom. When I asked him to, he would say, "Why? You're my wife."

When I thought about my marriage, I could hear my mother's voice, saying, "You've made your bed. Now lie in it."

I had that trapped feeling again where I felt my heart was being squeezed by a big hand. I couldn't breathe and I would chant in my head, *forget it, forget it* until the feelings went away. I wished I had someone to talk to. I wished I had the courage to get out of the marriage, but I didn't see a way to fully support myself. I knew I couldn't go home, so I shoved all my thoughts to somewhere in my head where I didn't have to think about it.

I found out I was pregnant after Tom left on a six-month cruise to Laos. In 1962 the likelihood of a war in Vietnam was heating up. One morning Tom told me that if he didn't come home, he would be gone, he would not know where he was going, and he would not know when he would be coming back.

He didn't come home for six months. I continued to work and save money. When he came home, he started drinking with his buddies every night. I never knew when to expect him. We continually argued about his drinking, his absences, and his refusal to even call to say when he'd be home.

I didn't know at the time that Tom was an alcoholic. I hadn't grown up around drinking so I knew nothing about alcoholism. Tom had been raised by his mother, who survived on welfare as she raised Tom and his eight siblings. His father was an alcoholic who lived somewhere in Arkansas. During my pregnancy, Tom's mother called and informed him that his father had been found dead in a train boxcar in Arkansas. Tom showed no emotion at the news. He told me he had few memories of his father. He remembered his father had come to Oregon once and was abusive toward his mother. His older brother and his friend threw him out of the house and threatened to kill him if he ever laid a hand on her again.

During high school both Tom and his brother made "home brew," but I thought it was just a thing boys did in high school. My dad had always said, "Don't marry a boy who drinks." I thought he was telling me this because Southern Baptists viewed drinking as a sin. Many years later I wondered if he had intended his statement to be a warning. But how could he have expected me to know about alcoholism?

I stayed with my job until I began my eighth month of pregnancy. My baby was due in late April (1963). Tom had served four years in the Navy and was due to be discharged in June. He told me we needed to give up the apartment and wanted me to live with my sister Barbara and her husband Harold in Huntington Beach until the baby arrived. We would find a new place to live after he was discharged. He didn't have any idea that I hated my brother-in-law or why living with the man who raped me as a child was the last thing in the world I wanted to do. Without enough money to keep our apartment, though, I felt trapped. We packed the car and my parakeet and drove to Huntington Beach.

Barbara and Harold had moved to California from Texas so that Harold could work as a computer programmer. Thankfully, he wasn't around during the day while I lived in their home. He liked to drink and often came home after I was in bed. There was very little said between us.

Tom had gone back to San Diego to live aboard the ship until he was discharged. Most of the young mothers who were neighbors of my sister came over in the morning for coffee after their husbands left for work. Much of the conversation centered on childbirth. No detail was spared about how horrible it was. Everyone seemed to be trying to outdo each other with their stories of pain and suffering. I didn't think I had been affected until I went into labor. Then I realized all those stories were still in my head. I was scared to death.

The birth of my baby was fraught with complications. I began to vomit repeatedly, which caused me to become dehydrated. I knew little about the process of birth but I heard the doctor say I was "dilated to four centimeters" and seemed to be "stuck" there. Ten hours later I dilated enough for the baby to be pulled out with forceps. My son Danny weighed five pounds, three ounces. I had a brief glimpse of him before they whisked him away. No one had talked to me about breastfeeding, so I just assumed bottle feeding was the appropriate thing to do.

As I look back upon this experience, I am appalled by the hospital's handling of the situation. They bound my breasts, which were very sore, making the pain worse. They told me they were giving me medication to dry up the milk. When I asked to see my baby, I was told he was in isolation because they were still trying to figure out what caused my vomiting during labor.

All the symptoms vanished after Danny's birth. I realized my intense fright had caused my body to react with vomiting. I still was unable to see him for another week. Finally, they brought him to me on the day I was discharged. I didn't know how I was going to be able to stand going back to my sister's house. Maybe I could just stay in my room with my baby and avoid Harold.

On the day I was discharged, my mother arrived to see me, the baby, and my sister Barbara. During the few days she visited, she told me the story of my birth.

I had been delivered at home by Dr. Butts, the rural doctor in the Red River Valley (the doctor who failed to file my birth certificate). It was well known that he had a drinking problem and often arrived at a home with liquor on his breath. Mother presented another obstacle for him, because as a God-fearing, modest woman, she would not let him look under the sheets when he delivered her children. He had to do it all "by feel." (I wondered when I heard this story if other women gave birth this way, too.)

Daddy paid Dr. Butts for my delivery with two of the plumpest chickens from Mother's flock and a big sack of potatoes.

Mother told me how difficult it was to keep me fed.

"When you were born, I was trying to wean Ben because my milk was drying up. I didn't have the milk to breastfeed you."

I was tiny, weighing about four pounds, my mother

guessed. (I was born at home and was not weighed.) She had to figure out some way to feed me or I would have died. She started by dipping a rag in diluted cow's milk and letting me suck on it. The next step was to get a bottle and some nipples to feed me, something that was not easily done in wartime due to rationing of many commodities, including rubber. Daddy was able to find a couple of nipples made out of black rubber, which were harder than the regular nipples that weren't readily available during World War II anyway.

Another challenge came from my brother Ben. He was not taking kindly to being weaned and kept taking my bottles and sucking all the milk out. Even when Mother placed me in a flatbed truck under a shade tree with my bottle propped up while she did chores, Ben would find a way to climb up and take my bottle.

My sister Barbara worried about whether or not I would survive. She later told me it was hard for her to think about anything else while at school. She didn't understand why our mother couldn't breastfeed me. Her version of the events surrounding my birth was different from my mother's, but somehow I survived my earliest (but not only) experience with near-starvation.

Now I had my own tiny baby, and I felt an overwhelming love for him. I panicked each time one of my nieces or my nephew hung over the bassinet to peer at him. I was terrified they would turn the bassinet over. I just wanted the two of us to stay in our room. Thinking about my baby kept me from thinking too much about being forced to stay in the same house with the man who had raped me. Still, I felt trapped and I knew I was totally dependent on Tom to get out of there.

Tom was due to be discharged in June, two months after Danny's birth. Every time I spoke to him about moving, he would say, "Well, where are we supposed to get the money?" I told him I would save my entire allotment for two months and pleaded with him to save what he could from his pay. We could use that money for rent.

In late May Barbara started driving me around to find a place to live. We finally found a house I thought Tom and I could afford. The rugs were filthy from the previous tenant's dogs, but I was optimistic that I could clean them. I had no furniture, no washer for diapers, no bed—nothing except a hand-me-down crib from Barbara and a playpen. Luckily, Barbara loaned me fifty dollars so I could buy her friend's couch and chair.

Getting a washer was my priority. There were no disposable diapers on the market at that time, but the back yard did have a clothesline I could use to dry clothes. I was glad I lived in sunny southern California. I bought a washer "on account" at Sears, even though I didn't know where the money for monthly payments was going to come from. I just fervently hoped Tom would be able to find a job after he was discharged.

I had been collecting thirty-one dollars a week from unemployment, but the military allotment would stop when Tom was discharged from the Navy. What were we going to do then?

Tom had been an electrician in the Navy, but he told me he had to join the electrician's union to work, which cost money. He began looking for something else to do. He was at a disadvantage because he had not been raised in a family that valued education and would work at any job available in order to put food on the table.

He found a job selling vacuum cleaners but it brought in very little money. We were late on rent, I didn't have any grocery money, and I didn't know what to do. I remembered seeing a six-pack of empty Coke bottles in my neighbor's garage, so I asked her if I could have them. She said yes but didn't ask why. I sold them for the nickel deposit and with my thirty cents, bought a jar of baby food for Danny. As hard up as we were for money, Tom still bought cigarettes. I had no idea about this addiction and couldn't understand why he would do such a thing. He just got mad if I said anything to him.

Thankfully, shortly after that Tom told me he had landed a job with Earl Schieb, a car painting company, and was going to earn a decent salary.

We settled into the house in Huntington Beach. At first we slept on the floor. After Tom received his first paycheck, we were able to buy a used bed and mattress. I had grocery money and Tom was going to work every day.

Maybe, I thought to myself, things would work out after all in this marriage.

It wasn't long, though, until Tom started going out after work to have "a few beers" with his buddies. I was hurt each time he did this, because he came home drunk. I told him how much I hated that he used our money to drink. We didn't have that kind of money. We always ended up in a big argument, with nothing solved. It took years for me to realize that it did no good to try to reason with him when he was drinking.

After Danny's birth I asked the doctor about birth control. The "pill" had just come out, and he gave me a prescription for a month's supply of pills. I took them faithfully, but I became so ill from vomiting and headaches that I had to stop. The pill was very strong back then, much more so than it is today. I tried another method—a spermicide foam—which worked for about nine months. Then I discovered I was pregnant again. I cried for a week before I told Tom. He didn't seem to care or want to think about the expense of having another child. I felt even more trapped, and it's possible he was feeling trapped also, because his drinking intensified.

My sister Barbara made plans to go back to work at the telephone company in Huntington Beach. She asked if I would babysit her two-year-old daughter, Sandra Kay. (Her older two children were in school.) I desperately needed the money, but when she told me her husband Harold would be dropping Sandy off in the morning, my heart sank to the bottom of my feet. I had thought I was finally free of him, but I wasn't.

I showed him how I felt about him every morning when he dropped off Sandy at my house. I took her inside, glared at him venomously, and slammed the door in his face, immediately locking it. After all, it was my house and my right to do it. I would have done worse if I could.

In the meantime I was looking for a way to make more money. I had heard from a neighbor that the owner of a small apartment complex a few miles away in Stanton was looking for someone to live in one of the units and manage the others. It meant free rent. I had never managed an apartment building, but I figured I could learn. I made Tom promise to come straight home from work and take me to the interview I had arranged. I think the free rent appealed to him because he did come straight home that night and took me to the interview. We were behind in our rent and the landlord was dropping around every week to try to collect it.

I was able to convince the owner that I could do the job of managing the apartments. The job consisted primarily of collecting the rent from the other tenants and reporting any needed repairs to the owner. I had to let the tenants know the rules and complete rental contracts when a new tenant moved in. I was ecstatic and couldn't wait to move. Barbara, however, was not happy about losing a babysitter. With the free rent, I no longer needed babysitting money. The real perk was that I didn't have to look at Harold's ugly face five days a week anymore.

Tom was unhappy with his job and with the help of a friend, he landed a job with Nationwide Safety Brake in Glendale, near Los Angeles. It was at least an hour's commute from our home in Stanton. We only had one car, so this meant I was stuck at home with a ten-month-old son while pregnant with another child.

I gave birth to a little girl and named her April Renee. It was another delivery with complications. My labor began time and again, then stopped. Finally, I was admitted to the hospital and labor was induced. Forceps were used, and it must have been traumatic for April, because after we went home she cried nonstop for almost a week. Nothing would soothe her. I could rarely get her and Danny to sleep at the same time, so I was worn out. When I looked at her, I felt overwhelming compassion because she was a girl. I knew she would have a hard life ahead of her.

After about a month Tom began coming home later and later. His excuse was that he was waiting for traffic to die down before driving home. He was often drunk when he arrived home, so I was worried he would be involved in an accident.

Then it happened. One Saturday night he decided to go out, driving to one of his drinking hangouts. Around midnight he was driving home and he crashed into someone who was backing out of a driveway onto the road he was traveling. The police estimated Tom was driving about fifty miles per hour on impact. The big V8 engine of our 1960 Impala was pushed almost inside the car. Tom sustained two broken legs and had several teeth knocked out, but he was alive. He was booked for driving under the influence, possession of an open container, and excessive speed. He was twenty-four years old and I had given birth to my second child only one month earlier.

A friend of mine took me to the hospital to pick him up three days later. I had my twenty-month-old son and baby daughter in tow. He was on disability for a few months, which barely provided enough money to live on. If we hadn't had the free rent, we couldn't have made it. When Tom was well enough to go back to work, he was immediately fired. I learned that he had been stealing parts from the shop and selling them. Once again, we were living on the edge.

Our good friend, Forrest Townsley, had moved from Huntington Beach to San Francisco, where he was working for a car painting company. He got Tom a job, so we loaded up the car we had bought to replace the wrecked one and a trailer and headed for northern California. Forrest had located an apartment for us in San Leandro, a less expensive place to live than San Francisco.

I hated San Leandro and the apartment complex where we lived. Danny was almost two years old and had no place to play. There wasn't anywhere I could walk to with two babies. I knew we had to get out of there. One of my neighbors subscribed to a newspaper and I asked her if I could have it when she was finished. There was an ad for a brake service man needed in Sacramento. Tom agreed to apply and got the job.

Another move, but I hoped it was to a better place.

9   TURNING POINT

I met Joanne the day we moved to Sacramento. I actually met three of her four children first. Seeing our rented trailer, the children came running across the street to see what was going on and ask questions. Eventually, a woman emerged from the house and walked over. There was nothing remarkable about her. She had mid-length brown hair, large hips, was a little overweight, and had a cigarette dangling between her fingers.

"My name's Joanne," she said. "These are my kids. I hope they're not bothering you."

Our families soon became friends.

Most weekends in the summer, we took family camping trips together. It was a cheap way to entertain the children and enjoy adult company. For the first time since marrying Tom, I felt as if I finally had a friend. Joanne and I shared babysitting and discussed child rearing, although neither one of us knew very much about it. We talked about future plans and dreams. We had both married young and the children had come quickly.

Eventually, both of our families moved to other neighborhoods, but we still remained friends.

I discovered I was pregnant again. I had started using

birth control pills because the doctor told me they were not as strong as the ones that had given me such severe side effects. I took them, but within a week I was nauseous, had headaches, and in general felt awful, so I had to stop. I had talked to Tom several times about getting a vasectomy, but he flat out refused. As much as I hated the diaphragm, I had to go back to using it. I ended up falling into the small percentage of women who got pregnant despite using the diaphragm.

I experienced certain calm with this pregnancy and was looking forward to my new baby's birth. I had a good gynecologist and because of my history, he kept a close watch on the baby's weight, hoping he would weigh no more than six pounds. When he thought the time was right, he induced labor.

My little baby arrived at six pounds, eight ounces, and he was eighteen inches long. He looked like a little butterball. I named him David Forrest. I chose Forrest as his middle name after the man who had been a good friend during some of the hardest times I'd experienced. David was the easiest and happiest baby out of my three children.

Before David's birth, I thought I might eventually figure out a way to divorce Tom, even though I didn't know how I could possibly make it on my own with two small children. Now I had *three* children, and divorce seemed impossible. I knew I couldn't support my children and myself on what I earned from terrible, low-paying jobs, and I had no faith in Tom's ability or willingness to pay child support. I resigned myself to the situation with Tom, realizing I needed time to figure out how to leave my marriage.

Then I was blindsided.

One Saturday morning Joanne's husband, Jim, called and asked for Tom. I told him Tom was at work.

"I don't think so," Jim responded quickly. "I think he and Joanne are together."

Stunned, it took me a minute to understand what he was

saying. Why would they be together? I began pummeling him with questions. Jim had overheard a phone conversation between Joanne and Tom. Joanne had arranged with her mom to babysit their four kids over the weekend. She told Jim she was driving to the Bay Area to visit a friend. Jim had called her friend, who knew of no such plans.

Jim was enraged and told me to get a babysitter for my kids so we could find Joanne and Tom. He thought they were somewhere on "the strip," a string of shady little motels along Highway 80 in Sacramento. He picked me up, then stopped and bought a six-pack of beer. I felt sick to my stomach, but opened a can anyway and took a few sips. Jim was cruising along the frontage road where all the motels were. He spotted Tom's black pickup parked at a small, cheap motel.

"I'm guessing they're in that room," Jim said between clenched teeth, pointing to the brownish red door with peeling paint directly in front of Tom's pickup. "And I don't think they're playing Canasta," he added.

He ordered me to get out and go with him. He hammered on the door with both fists, calling Joanne's name. "Open the door or I'll call the cops!" he kept yelling.

Finally the door opened. Tom stood there solemnly. Joanne looked at us guiltily from the back of the small room. Suddenly, I saw a Coors beer can hurtling toward her. It struck her chest and foaming beer flowed down her blouse. I looked at my hands and saw that I was no longer holding my can of beer. I stumbled back to the car, begging Jim to get in and go. Jim demanded that Joanne get in his car, but she refused.

I was numb. The word "betrayal" kept knocking around in my head. Every waking moment, I relived that awful and devastating scene. I couldn't unsee it. I kept thinking, What is friendship? Must it end in deceit and betrayal? Where is this all going? What am I going to do? I had no answers.

My trust in Tom was destroyed. I felt shattered.

Tom begged me to forgive him. He vowed his love for me and said he would never do anything like that again. We cobbled the marriage back together. In my head I kept thinking maybe I could change things and we could have a good marriage. Maybe we just needed more stability and that would fix things between us. But in my heart I knew I was only buying time.

I longed to buy a house. Tom was eligible for a loan from the Veterans Administration, and no down payment would be required. I found a job working from 4:00 p.m. to midnight with the California Almond Growers, sorting almonds on a conveyer belt. I hired a neighbor to watch the kids for two hours a day until Tom got home from work. He had started coming home after work, which allowed the babysitter to leave. This gave us added income to help with buying a house. I found a nice house with a huge back yard where the kids could play and I could plant a garden. It was in an older neighborhood and the location wasn't the greatest, but it was a house we could afford.

My job was seasonal and I was relieved when it ended. I had broken out in a rash up and down my legs and on my arms from the dust coming off the conveyer belt. The roar of the machines was so loud that the employees wouldn't have been able to hear even if we tried to talk to each other. We had not been advised to wear masks or ear plugs.

Mother had always taught me how to can food and be frugal. I threw myself into growing a garden, canning vegetables, making homemade soups, and freezing vegetables when I ran out of jars and lids. I started watching a couple of children during the day and after school to earn a little income for myself. Tom's drinking had intensified. Sometimes he stayed out all night. We fought a lot and had very little communication other than arguing. I knew I had to make some kind of decision about how I was going to get out of the marriage, whether it was right away or later.

I had saved a lot of the grocery money Tom gave to me and the entire babysitting money, and I finally had enough money to buy a little secondhand Opal station wagon. I wouldn't have to wait until Tom got home from work to shop for groceries, plus I could take the kids out to a park to play on the swings. I tried to pretend that life was normal. I still didn't realize I was married to an alcoholic. I kept thinking that if I could just do better, Tom would be happier and would not drink anymore. On one occasion I tried to stop him from going out to the bars by taking his car keys and telling him I had flushed them down the toilet. (I hadn't.) He went out and sat in the driver's seat of his truck. Then he repeatedly opened his door and smashed in the passenger door of my car, which was parked next to his. He was a mean drunk.

I finally figured out how I was going to escape my marriage and build a new life.

Education. That was going to be my way out.

It was 1968, and I had given eight years of my life to Tom and our marriage for the sake of our children. Now Danny was starting kindergarten and April was eligible for Head Start (a government preschool). I had enough money saved from babysitting other people's children to hire my own babysitter for six-month-old David so that I could attend classes at the local community college.

I was ecstatic. I met with a college counselor and planned my class schedule. I could only attend classes on Tuesdays and Thursdays. That way I didn't have to hire a sitter on Mondays, Wednesdays, and Fridays. When a class was full, I put my name on the waitlist, sitting in until someone dropped out and the professor announced an opening. This method worked about 90 percent of the time.

Sleep, blessed sleep. That's what I wanted most during this time. I soon discovered I could get very little schoolwork done during the day with the responsibilities of the children, the house, and meals. My nights were also filled with taking care of the kids, as Tom made it clear it was my place to be home at all times unless I was out making money. He continued to go out at night and drink. I usually stayed up until one or two in the morning, trying to finish my homework. At 6:00 a.m. I got up after just a few hours of sleep, dressed and fed the children, and waited for David's sitter to arrive. I took my other two children to school and went on to my full morning of classes. Tom continued to insist that I fix him breakfast every morning, slamming the door on his way out to work. I didn't challenge him about breakfast because even though I wanted a divorce, I still felt as if our awful marriage was somehow my fault.

Even though I had little time to get my schoolwork done, I refused to take fewer than fifteen units per semester. I was determined to finish school as quickly as possible. I never knew when Tom was going to be home, and when he was home, he was getting meaner. I realized he didn't like my going to school at all. Did he suspect this might become a way out of our marriage for me? It was possible.

I loved the biological sciences and wanted to go to nursing school ultimately, but I soon realized obtaining a teaching credential would be a more realistic choice. I could be home during the summers with the children and have more time with them after school. I didn't have the gumption to look into how little a teaching job paid at that time.

After two years of college, things got so bad with Tom that I had finally had enough. I told him to leave. This occurred one night when he came home from drinking (which was certainly the wrong time). A huge yelling scene occurred, waking the children, who began crying. Tom punched a hole in the wall with his fist and shouted, "You will never make it without me."

I didn't say another word. I was stunned when the

meaning of his words sank in. It sounded to me like he didn't want a divorce, but I certainly was going after one as soon as I could. I got the kids calmed down and back in bed. I grabbed a blanket and slept on the couch for a few hours before my day started again.

That morning I did not fix breakfast for Tom.

A friend gave me the name of her divorce lawyer and I made an appointment. When I walked into the lawyer's office, I announced, "I need to file for a divorce." I was twenty-six years old.

The lawyer, Mr. Saldine, informed me that I had to pay a retainer. I didn't have any money so he asked me what I did have besides three children. I offered him the new RC Victor stereo console Tom had purchased without discussing it with me. Mr. Saldine said, "Fine. It will probably look good in this office. Have a seat."

Our house was put on the market and sold in four weeks. Tom and I each came out with fifteen hundred dollars. Out of ignorance, I hadn't listed the house with an agent, but my choice ended up saving me from paying a commission. I wanted to buy another house, the first house I would own by myself, so I found a realtor named Gino Beatty. "I have fifteen hundred dollars to put down on a house," I told him. When I told him how much my monthly income was, he laughed. "I can't find you anything for that," he said.

"If you are any kind of realtor, you will," I said. "I will not take my kids to a cockroach-infested apartment and pay almost as much rent as I would for my own house."

I didn't have any idea how this would happen, but I was desperate. My job as a teacher's aide paid very little money, and Tom wasn't yet paying any child support.

Thankfully, Gino and the gods were looking out for me. He found a small house in Fair Oaks, a nice suburb of Sacramento. A young couple had purchased it only a year-and-a-half earlier, but the husband was in the military and had been transferred out of state. My down payment was accepted and I was able to assume their loan. My monthly mortgage payment was two hundred thirty-two dollars. I thought I was in heaven.

Gino gave me a potted azalea and said, "Good luck. You're the gutsiest woman I've ever met."

I told him he was the best realtor I had ever met. Of course, he was also the only one.

10 ON MY OWN

L ife was good. I was attending school, worked part time during the day, and was able to spend evenings with the kids. Danny was now in school more hours during the day and April was in preschool. I had a babysitter for David.

We were getting by with very little in the way of groceries and clothing. I didn't know anything about food stamps or welfare. I know now that my children would have had enough food to eat if I had known about these programs. I was just thankful April was able to get breakfast and lunch at Head Start, which was a government-funded program for low-income parents.

I was consumed by needing to finish school and getting a good job to provide a better life for my children. Often, they were forced to go to school in the rain wearing tennis shoes, then sit in class with wet feet.

Tom had moved in with Joanne and her four children. He had visitation rights every other weekend, but he took the kids sporadically. I had no love for Joanne, the woman my husband had cheated on me with, but I figured my kids would at least be able to have better meals when they stayed there.

Tom had been ordered to pay child support of two hundred forty dollars per month, but I rarely saw the money. Rumor had it that Joanne's ex-husband had injured himself on the job and wasn't working, so she wasn't getting any child support for her four children. Tom had apparently realized that his life with another woman hadn't turned out to be what he had imagined. One weekend he brought the kids back home and I invited him in. I asked him for money to buy milk. He slapped a twenty-dollar bill on the kitchen counter and said, "You won't make it without me. I will starve you out of that idea." I had heard that before and it made me even more resolute in obtaining my freedom from him.

I was stunned. I had no idea he still wanted to be with me. When he left, I began seething. Didn't he care about his children at all? If I starved, they would starve, too.

In spite of what Joanne had done to me, I wanted to give friendship another try. I met a master teacher at the school where I worked, and we became good friends. Kathleen's husband worked as a buyer for the Navy commissary. He was given lots of food samples, which Kathleen just tossed into her freezer. The samples mostly consisted of breaded fish sticks, breaded shrimp, and frozen dinners. She and her husband didn't eat breaded food and her cats were the recipients of the fish.

One day I told her about my situation and confessed, "I don't know what I will do when I have to quit my job to student teach."

The next day she came over with the trunk of her green Javelin filled with frozen breaded fish sticks, shrimp, frozen dinners, and cereal. I couldn't believe her generosity. The kids loved the food. She told me she would continue to bring food over and told me not to worry about having to quit work to student teach.

I don't know if she ever fully realized how grateful I was for what she did. Kathleen and I remained friends for forty years until she passed away. Her daughter requested that I write her eulogy.

I was still driving my little Opal and had begun student teaching. One morning the car wouldn't start and my neighbor said it had a dead battery. I began panicking because I didn't have any money to buy a new battery and I absolutely had to get my student teaching completed. My neighbor jumped my battery so I could get to work. After class I went out to the parking lot, crossing my fingers that my car would start. It didn't. The teacher who had been supervising me kindly jumped the battery. This situation continued for about a week. The only way for me to be able to buy a battery was to let utility bills go unpaid with the hope that I could catch up later. I managed to feed my children, though, with the food my friend had brought for them.

The years spent trying to finish my four-year degree had been tough, no doubt about it. When I received my provisional teaching credential and signed my first contract for $6,800 per year, though, I was thrilled by what I had managed to accomplish.

We were still living below the poverty line but I was making progress.

In California a fifth year of education was required to have a full teaching credential. I decided to combine my fifth year of education with earning a master's degree. Teachers earned raises based on years of service and degrees obtained, and I needed those raises. Having both a credential and a master's would allow my family to have a better standard of living. That's when I hit another roadblock, as the rules didn't allow for the fifth year to be counted toward a graduate degree. Additional hurdles were taking the Graduate Record Exam (GRE), applying to my program of choice, and getting accepted into the program.

I petitioned the college and was told that if I could successfully challenge certain courses, take the remaining required courses, and complete a thesis, I could take the shortcut. I gladly accepted, even though I had no idea whether I had the knowledge to challenge the courses. And I didn't even fully understand what a "thesis" was.

By the grace of God, I was able to pass the courses.

I taught summer school to survive financially. There was no end to my children's complaining about having to attend summer school, too, but it solved my problem of what to do with them during that time and I figured it wouldn't hurt them. To appease them I took them to the local A&W every Friday for a root beer float and a hamburger.

I wondered at times how much longer I could put myself under the stress of teaching, going to school at night, taking care of the kids, and paying all the bills. But I knew there had to be light at the end of the tunnel if I could just hang in there.

Even though I was busy, I had been dating a man who met the criteria of liking my children. He was thirty-four, had a degree from the University of California, Davis (UC Davis) and worked as an underwriter for an insurance company. He had never been married, but he was family-oriented and we enjoyed a lot of outings with his mother, brother, and sister. I thought I was in love with him and when he proposed, I said yes.

I still had no firm basis upon how to choose a partner, so I didn't realize that I was marrying him for the wrong reasons. The marriage lasted five years. I had learned from my first marriage that sticking with the wrong relationship didn't work. It wasn't his fault. He had done all the right things, even typing my master's degree thesis. I just came to realize I didn't love him. To stay in the marriage wouldn't have been fair to either one of us.

I was alone again, but the time I had devoted to securing a professional career had enabled me to provide for my children on my own. I really enjoyed teaching and being able to have summers off to do things with my children.

Things were still rocky between my children's father and me. My ex-husband tried to communicate with me through our oldest son. I resented Dan being used as a go-between. One day Dan announced that Tom and Joanne were getting married. It was the Christmas holiday season and Tom had the kids for the weekend, so I took the opportunity to go Christmas shopping. As I was browsing the aisles of a department store, I looked up and saw my daughter. She ran over when I called to her. A moment later Joanne appeared. I was unsure what to say, so I decided to congratulate her on her forthcoming marriage.

"Thank you," she replied.

For the first time in my life, I thought of something to say on the spur of the moment.

"Remember," I said, "he has that fatal flaw."

Joanne smiled smugly. "Oh? What's that?"

"He cheats on his wife!" I said. Before she could respond, I turned and left, not even waiting for her reaction. I was proud of myself for speaking up, something I'd never been able to do before, especially on the spur of the moment.

11 SAYING GOODBYE

It was time to reassess my life. I had finished school and earned my full teaching credential. My children were growing up fast. It had been a long road to get to this point. I recalled a meeting I had with a banker during leaner times, when I tried to explain to him that I only had money for half the house payment but could give him what I had. He had refused to take my money and had laughed me right out of the bank. I decided I was never going to feel humiliated ever again for not being able to pay a bill. And I would never show my ignorance again either, if at all possible.

I started planning a trip to Eugene, Oregon, where my parents still lived. My children would be able to see their grandparents, as well as my brother and his family. Always frugal, I also planned to buy the kids' school clothes for the upcoming year because in Oregon we would not have to pay sales tax on our purchases. It would be our big summer treat.

The last time I had seen my parents was when I told my mother I was getting a divorce.

"Can't you wait until the children are grown?" she had asked. This hurt me deeply and I felt much guilt about making the choice to divorce. She had no idea what it had been like for my children and me to live with an alcoholic. I was the first of her four children to get a divorce, and she didn't speak to me for a couple of years. She viewed my divorce as a reflection on her upbringing of me. Later, much to her chagrin, both my sister Barbara and my brother Ben also divorced their spouses. I guess none of us had believed in the old adage Mother liked to repeat: *You've made your bed, now lie in it.*

I had been happy when Barbara divorced her husband, Harold. Not only was he my rapist, he was also an abusive alcoholic. Barbara had tried waiting until her kids were grown, but it was her own children who kept telling her, "Mom, you need to divorce Dad."

I guess Mother forgave me for the divorce because we did have a nice visit when I brought my children to Oregon. Mostly I spent time with my brother Gerald and his family. It was more comfortable than spending time around Daddy, who still said very little to me. Neither my mother nor my father mentioned my graduation from college or all I had done to provide for myself and my children.

We returned home to California and I began dating again. I wasn't interested in getting married. I just wanted to have someone to go out to the movies or dinner with, someone I could enjoy being around, someone who would like doing activities with my children.

My children were older now, and I didn't worry so much about them liking the men I dated. And they didn't. Not a single one. When the doorbell rang, one of the kids would open the door, turn around, and walk off. They all did the same thing. Finally, after several months, I decided to have it out with them.

"You expect me to like your friends and I am expecting the same of you," I said. I explained that my plan was not to get married but to have someone to do things with—just like they did things with their friends. Things got a little better, but there were always snide remarks. Danny called one of the men a homosexual the entire time I dated him. Sometimes I wondered if it was even worth it to date.

In 1978 I applied for a job as an administrator with the County Office of Education in Placerville, California. I'll never forget that interview. The county superintendent's last question was "Can you milk a goat?"

Needless to say, I got the job. We moved to Rescue, California, a small town nine miles west of Placerville. Our house sat upon five acres of land. April wanted a horse and Danny and David were happy to join 4H.

David was still in elementary school, but Danny and April were teenagers, so they started doing the stupid things teenagers do. Fifteen-year-old April started seeing an eighteen-year-old boy with a police record. I forbade her to see him, but she would just sneak out her bedroom window after I went to sleep. She saw him after school and even skipped school sometimes in order to be with him all day. She refused to obey my rules and we fought constantly.

Finally she informed me that her father, Tom, had told her she could live with him in Sacramento. She would not have to obey my rules there. Of course that option was the one she chose. I was hurt but had no control over whether she moved out or not. I did try to warn her that she would be the outsider in Tom's family, since Joanne had four other children. It wasn't long before she realized I had been right. She was the outsider.

Instead of returning home, though, she elected to move in with her new boyfriend. At least he had the decency to bring her to see me and ask my permission. I was between a rock and a hard place. April was only sixteen, but if I said no, she would do it anyway. I made them promise she would finish high school, and they agreed, but I checked in with her later only to find out that she wasn't going to school. She told me, "I don't like taking the bus. Bob works and I don't have a car." So I bought her a car as a bribe.

She returned and finished high school.

As for my son Danny, he was staying out at night and drinking, which worried me to no end. By that time I had learned enough about alcoholism to know that he probably had a predisposition to becoming an alcoholic because of his father's, grandfather's, and several uncles' addictions. He was nearly eighteen years old and trying to talk to him about his drinking didn't seem to make any difference. He did manage to hold down a part-time job at Long's drugstore while attending high school. I encouraged him to attend community college, as I had, and after graduation he moved out and started taking classes.

My youngest child, David, had to spend a lot of time alone because of my long hours. I also had to go out of town several times a month for two days at a time. I feared I was losing control of him, too. Once when I was out of town, a friend told me he had seen David hitchhiking along the highway. I was devastated. Somehow we struggled through and he finished high school. He worked for a couple of years and then told me he was joining the Navy.

I cried all night. George H.W. Bush was ramping up for the Gulf War and I knew David would be involved. He was stationed aboard the aircraft carrier, USS *Ranger*, and he spent time in the Arabian Gulf, watching the oil wells burn and breathing in the toxins. When the *Ranger* was relieved of its duty in the Gulf, it sailed to ports in Japan, Korea, Australia, and back to San Diego.

David felt the military helped him to "grow up" and enabled him to see countries he would never have had the opportunity to see had it not been for his four years in the Navy. His biggest thrill was climbing Mount Fuji.

El Dorado County was very rural, with thirteen school districts that extended as far as South Lake Tahoe. In my job I was required to travel to all the districts and supervise some of their programs. Needless to say, I became very well acquainted with the superintendents (all male) and many school principals (majority male).

Some of these men seemed to think I was fair game for sexual harassment. During the holidays I was expected to attend parties that were often given in an administrator's home. I had three children at home and preferred to be home with them, but I reluctantly attended these events.

At one party I arrived late to find that most people had been drinking quite a bit. I poured a glass of wine and mingled with everyone, thinking that I could soon make my escape and go home. As I took my empty wine glass to the kitchen, I turned around to find the superintendent who was hosting the party standing in front of me. He took my shoulders, backed me up against the counter, and began kissing me, putting his tongue in my mouth.

I pushed him away and said, "Someone could walk in here and see this. I need to leave and go home."

He left and returned to the party.

I had to walk a fine line when such incidents occurred. I didn't feel as if I could damage any egos or react in an angry way or I would have been fired. I couldn't tell my boss because he had offended me also. All these incidents caused me emotional anguish. I began to ask myself why men felt as if they could do these things to me. A young, attractive female colleague in one of the districts told me the same thing frequently happened to her. She, too, felt that she could not say anything to her administrator for fear of losing her job.

The harassment only stopped when I began a relationship with a coworker.

I had never planned to remarry, but eventually I became engaged to a psychologist who, like me, worked for the county office. A new superintendent had been elected and he wanted to bring in his own management team. This meant all administrators were slated to lose their jobs. My fiancée's job was not in jeopardy, but mine was.

One evening we discussed the situation. "I don't know

why you are so worried," he said. "Move in with me and I will take care of you."

I stared at him for a moment, then got up and walked out of his house. His remarks had revealed to me that he had no appreciation of who I truly was, what I had been through, and how hard I had worked to become an administrator in a world of "good old boys." When a mutual friend later told me my fiancée had no idea why I had left him, I felt it proved my point that he didn't really know me at all.

I had struggled so hard to lift myself out of poverty, doing whatever was necessary to become independent and be able to take care of my children, battling constant feelings of guilt that I was not spending more time with them, blaming myself for their mistakes. And he just expected me to walk away from who I had become to be "taken care of"? I couldn't do it. I didn't *want* to do it.

I applied for jobs around the state and was finally hired by the University of California, Berkeley as a counselor. It wasn't an administrative job, but it was one that intrigued me. I started that job in 1985.

Four months later my brother called and told me our father was dying.

Daddy had been sick a long time. He had been given a blood transfusion during a hip replacement and received Hepatitis C-tainted blood. This occurred before blood was being screened thoroughly prior to being used in transfusions. Daddy's liver was slowly being destroyed.

I took time off on three occasions when my brother thought Daddy's death was imminent. When Daddy finally did die, I wasn't able to arrive until later in the day. I was heartbroken I hadn't been there to say goodbye before he passed. I stayed for his funeral and was able to see my sister Barbara, who came from Texas. We both tried to comfort Mother as best we could, but she was inconsolable.

"I'm ready to join him anytime in heaven. I don't have anything else to do on this earth." Mother went on to live seventeen more years, but she always maintained that she was ready to join Daddy any day.

I wished my relationship with my father had been closer. He had rarely spoken to me, but when he did, he was not unkind. Usually if he said something, I listened. I had always assumed he talked to my two brothers more than me, but when I mentioned this to my brother Gerald, he said Daddy hadn't talked to them much, either. Apparently the Runyan men just didn't talk very much.

I returned home after the funeral and threw myself into my work.

12 BERKELEY

As a counselor at the University of California, Berkeley (or UC Berkeley, as it was called), my caseload consisted of all students who were admitted under the designation of "Learning Disability" (LD) or "Attention Deficit Hyperactivity Disorder" (ADHD). Section 504 of the Rehabilitation Act of 1973 stated that people with disabilities had the right to attend college and be accommodated. While working for the County Office of Education, I had been in charge of the "Low Incidence" programs. These were the programs that served all disabilities, and my experience was one of the qualifying reasons I had been hired as a counselor at UC Berkeley.

I loved working for the university and seeing all the things I had never been exposed to before. It wasn't unusual to see unconventional happenings. One of the more memorable ones was the time helicopters circled above the university for an entire day. The media was hoping that if chaos broke out, they would immediately know about it. That morning the chancellor, who lived on campus, had discovered a makeshift shanty attached to his front door. In 1985 apartheid—the policy of race-based discrimination and segregation—was being protested, and it was well known that the university's retirement system had invested heavily in South African mines. The students had taken up this cause and wanted the retirement system investments pulled out of South Africa. The hope was that the protest would show the world that the U.S. did not believe in discrimination based on race. This was only one of many causes that were protested on campus during the time I worked there.

Witnessing the many protests about various causes on campus caused me to think deeply about world matters and the freedom for students to take up such causes. My world was expanding, and I loved it.

One of the accommodations that students with learning disabilities were entitled to was extra time on exams. As an educator, I was well aware that these students (who fell under the umbrella of "dyslexic") were slower-than-normal readers.

Due to this disability, a dyslexic student's brain functioned in a way that would only enable him or her to decode one word at a time instead of a whole sentence. When the student finished decoding every word in a paragraph, he or she would then have to go back and reread the entire paragraph to grasp its meaning. This took extra time, and some professors balked at allowing this accommodation of extra time. They maintained that anyone would do better with extra time to take an exam.

Since I was only a "counselor" and did not have a Ph.D., my word wasn't worth much. I realized that if I wanted to remain at UCB, get fair treatment for my students, and be validated as a person who knew what I was talking about, a Ph.D. was a requirement.

There were some faculty members, however, who were willing to spend about thirty minutes listening to what I had to say. I carefully prepared my presentation. I began my remarks by citing research on the reading difficulty the students had. Then I launched into the topic of "dysgraphia," the inability to write legibly, and the need for the student to have an oral exam or a scribe. I showed an overhead of the writing of a Berkeley student who had dysgraphia. It literally looked like chicken scratches and was unreadable. I explained this was caused by a neurological disorder called "visual motor integration." This sample of handwriting was the very best this student could do.

One of the professors raised her hand and asked, "Couldn't someone just sit down with him and teach him how to write?"

This was the level of understanding most of these professors had. They didn't realize that this student had spent many years with teachers and private tutors, trying to improve his visual motor integration. This was the disability. This student was also gifted, as many of my counselees were.

I needed the validation of the professors if I was going to be taken seriously on this subject. What was the best way to do this? Could I really get a Ph.D.? I thought about how hard it had been to earn an undergraduate degree, as well as a master's degree. I told myself I would be able to do that again in order to get a Ph.D. My children were out of the house this time, so why not give it a try?

It's a good thing I was too naïve to comprehend how hard it was going to be. I found out that even though I had a master's and had taken the Graduate Record Exam (GRE), it had been more than five years, so I had to take the GRE again. This was a shock and I almost gave up the entire idea. I had never been very good at taking lengthy, timed exams with multiple subjects. I figured I would probably do okay on the verbal part, but I would certainly need to bone up on math. I was relieved to learn that the logic section of the exam would not count. Whew. I could never figure out those problems. My strategy would be to guess on that section. I hired a tutor to help me with math.

The day arrived and I was cold with fear. Once I had made up my mind to apply for the Ph.D. program, I didn't want anything to stop me. I took the test and left afterwards feeling sick to my stomach. The results would take a few weeks.

In the meantime I had to interview before a committee. That was the easy part. I had been a teacher, dealing with special needs children, and also an administrator. I figured I could prove I was worthy of being accepted into the program. My GRE scores had not been posted before the interview.

Only seven people were admitted into the program that year, and I was one of them. I was on top of the world.

Then my scores came in. I had performed in the ballpark on verbal and math. I had guessed at every answer in the logic section, not even reading the questions, yet logic turned out to be my second highest score. My overall score was not stellar. I had never believed that putting high stakes on test scores for admitting students to programs was a good indicator of success, and my scores certainly supported my belief.

Now came the really hard part. I was back to working and attending school, trying to earn another degree. My department hired a friend of mine half time to take over some of my counseling duties so that I could dive into the program with a full course load and still work. One of the first classes I had to take was five units of upper-level statistics. My weakest skill. I had been told that the teacher in the fall was incredibly hard on students. If he sensed a weakness, he honed in on it like a shark after blood.

I decided it might be better to take the summer class. What a dumb idea. It was fast-paced and within two weeks I was hopelessly lost. Fortunately, my tutor had majored in statistics and he got me back on track. I passed the class and the lab with a B. In a doctoral program, if you get below a B-, you can be dismissed from the program. Failing was not an option for me.

I was on my way. In the meantime, controversy still raged on over providing students with learning disabilities extra time on exams. Most professors believed that anyone could do better with extra time.

I searched the literature and found only one study that researched the outcome of students with learning disabilities when put under strict time constraints on reading versus students without such disabilities. This was an unpublished dissertation. I knew what I had to do.

I began a small pilot study using students in my caseload to look at the difference between their timed reading scores and their extra time scores. I compared them with a group of students at Berkeley who did not have learning disabilities. The outcome: students with learning disabilities improved their scores dramatically when they were allowed fifty percent more time on the test (essentially, time-and-one-half).

Students without learning disabilities did not dramatically improve their test scores with extra time, however. They didn't need it. They could finish the test under the normal time limits.

The extra time scores for students with learning disabilities and students without learning disabilities were comparable. This showed that given the extra time to compensate for slower reading, the students with learning disabilities performed as well as regular university students. The study refuted the idea that "anyone" would do better with extra time.

One of the professors on my committee suggested that I measure the eye movements of students with learning disabilities when they were reading and compare those eye movements with those of normal-reading students. The School of Optometry had the equipment to do this. The results supported my theory that students with learning disabilities were slow, inefficient readers. They had many more backward saccadic eye movements. This meant that they were constantly looking back at words to decode them. Of course, this slowed their reading speed and comprehension significantly.

Dr. Sally Shaywitz at Yale University heard about my study. She was a neurological pediatrician and an advocate for students with nonvisible disabilities. She invited me to share the results of my small pilot study at Harvard University.

I couldn't believe it when the call came in from Dr. Shaywitz. It was exciting because I felt this small study vindicated students with learning disabilities (LDs). I remembered all the times that my students with LDs who were mainstreamed into regular classes were kept in at recess because they were unable to finish their work. I thought about all the adult students who took exams to get into professional schools, students whose dreams were dashed because they could not complete the exams under the time limits.

Then fear set in. What if my study wasn't good enough? I spent hours poring over the results, checking and rechecking numbers. I finally swallowed my fear and boarded the plane to present my research.

In attendance were professionals working in disability departments at the other Ivy League colleges. After the presentation, Sally and I talked. She asked if I would submit the study for publication in the *Journal of Learning Disabilities*. She went on to speak about the resistance of professors in allowing students extra time if they came into the university with a designated learning disability and testing showed that they needed that time. The issue was a hotbed of controversy throughout the university and college systems.

I submitted the study. I had never published anything

before and was thrilled when it was approved. After the study was published, word of it spread throughout the educational system. Of course, the study was critiqued by professors in academia to find flaws in the study. The biggest flaw—and certainly a valid one—was the size of the study. The sample size of forty students was too small. I decided that my dissertation would be on a much larger group of students, which would make the results more likely to be accepted.

It was during this time period that my mother, still living with my brother Gerald in Oregon, fell and broke her hip. She needed a hip replacement, but the doctors decided to pin her hip instead of replacing it. Gerald and I had no way of knowing that her hip bone was too fragile to maintain pins, so we agreed. The pins didn't hold, but the doctors still refused to perform a hip replacement. It was hard to see my ninety-year-old mother in so much pain when the second operation—another attempt to pin her hip—failed and left her in excruciating pain.

When the doctors did finally agree to a hip replacement, Mother picked up a staph infection in the hospital. Her hip became infected and they removed the replacement. Now she was virtually bedridden, spending all her time either in bed or in a wheelchair, unable to do anything except read and feed herself. Gerald and I were forced to put her in a residential care house, where she remained until her organs gave out three years later and she passed away at age ninety-three.

My brother Gerald, his wife, Mary, and I were all gathered around her bed when the time came. I could see the sun going down as I looked out her window. *My mother is going down, too,* I thought. I leaned over her and said, "Mother, it's okay. You will be with Daddy in heaven." She was not fully conscious, but she understood. She took one last breath and was gone. The composure of her face completely changed and became peaceful. I could feel peace flooding my body, too. I turned and looked out the window. The sun had completely set.

When I turned back to look at her, I saw her spirit leave her body in the shape of a white dove, flying away and disappearing. I knew then that I could still talk to my mother. I asked Gerald and Mary if they had seen it and they said no. Did I really see it, or did I just imagine it? Twenty years later I still see that image in my mind's eye, and I still talk to my mother.

13 PERSEVERANCE

I had heard the attrition rate in a doctoral program was fifty percent. It is designed to be so. I think most professors who are in charge of the doctoral candidates consider themselves the gatekeepers. If a professor doesn't like a candidate, they can make the process miserable and make it very difficult for the candidate to obtain the degree.

I had heard horror stories about the woman who became my advisor. She was head of the psychology department and had previously upheld the decision of one of the professors in her department to refuse a student with learning disabilities extra time. Yet she was known as the specialist in learning disabilities and attention deficit disorder. She also knew of my publication in the *Journal of Learning Disabilities*. I knew this professor was not an advocate for this group of people, but I didn't know how to fight for a different advisor.

My first meeting, where I presented my planned dissertation, was a disaster and she "blackballed" me. I pitched the idea of replicating my pilot study with a much bigger population. I emphasized how critical the study was. Laws had been passed mandating the provision of appropriate accommodations for students with disabilities at the university level. Accommodations were key to their success. The practice of replicating studies to see if the results are the same is the accepted way to validate studies. I could not believe that she was denying me the opportunity.

I was devastated, but I refused to accept this turn of events. I arranged to meet with one of my most respected professors and found myself crying as I explained the situation. Fortunately, he was aware of the actions of the person in question and knew of cases where she had unfairly kept deserving students from completing the program and obtaining a Ph.D. I heeded his advice: "Lay low, don't show your face in her department or office, and I'll find you an advisor."

Since I had been blackballed with all the professors in the psychology department who were advisors for Ph.D. candidates, he found a professor in the education department who was willing to meet with me to decide if he would be my advisor. At our meeting I explained my long history with LD and ADHD students and my role as a counselor for the students attending UC Berkeley. I gave him a copy of the journal in which my pilot study had been published and emphasized the critical need for this kind of research. I let him know that my article was being published as a chapter in a textbook written by Dr. Shaywitz at Yale University.

He agreed to become my advisor. I was so relieved to be able to continue in the program and felt the gods were watching over me.

I completed the "white paper," which essentially laid out the research study and design for my dissertation. I had chosen to replicate my previous study. I needed to get past one more hurdle, the dissertation committee of six. They approved the white paper, each making a suggestion on how best to structure the study. One professor wanted me to get IQ scores on my non-LD group. I explained that students accepted into college did not come with IQ scores, whereas I already had them for the LD group. (It had been part of the assessment battery to identify a learning disability.) The professor held firm and I dared not argue, even though I knew I had no way of gathering that data. I could only rely on research if it existed.

Performing an empirical study required approval from the department for the use of human subjects in research. A few weeks later I received the approval to perform the study. I was overjoyed.

I began my selection of volunteer students who did not have learning disabilities. Their duty was to provide me information that ruled out any kind of a learning disability, any special services such as speech therapy, or any special help from grammar school through high school. If selected, they would take a twenty-minute reading comprehension test. Each student was paid twenty-five dollars. I didn't want to take any chances that I would not have enough volunteers to perform my study. I was well aware that many students could use a little extra money, plus they would be able to learn how they performed in reading comprehension when compared to other college students.

Since I was still working part time, I met with all my subjects after work. It took me a lot longer to collect the data needed than I had anticipated, but at long last I had it. I was ready to run the statistical analysis on both groups to identify any significant differences in their scores. I found someone to help me with the program that I used to run the statistical analysis. Finally, all the information that was needed to write my dissertation had been gathered and analyzed.

I had been under the illusion that the head of my dissertation committee would monitor my chapters as I wrote the dissertation, but I soon found out otherwise. He required that I finish the dissertation before he would look at it. I suspected he had more doctoral students than he had time for, and I was filled with foreboding about not receiving any ongoing feedback. What if I had to revise the whole thing after he reviewed it?

After three months of compiling data, completing a statistical analysis, and drawing conclusions from the study, I was finally ready to submit it to him.

I was especially nervous about one aspect of my study—the issue of the regular university students' IQs. The professor who would be looking at my study was the same professor who wanted the IQ scores of the regular students included in the study. I suspected his suggestion originated because he had questions about the IQs of the UC Berkeley students with learning disabilities included in the study. He was also the chair of my dissertation committee. He may have thought them to be lower than the control group's collective IQs. This was strictly a guess on my part.

I had informed the entire committee about the criteria for being diagnosed with a learning disability such as reading, math, or written language. First and foremost, the individual had to score average or above average on a standardized IQ test. This ruled out low-IQ individuals. Most of the students with learning disabilities who were attending the university had a solid average or above-average IQ (and some scored in the range of gifted). This was most likely true of the control group.

The professor had my dissertation for three weeks before requesting a meeting with me. I was on pins and needles. At our meeting he began by complimenting me on the organization and analysis of my study, the statistics I had used, and the overall quality of my writing. I was beginning to lose that feeling of foreboding. Then he picked up a pencil, looked directly at me, and said, "I requested the IQ scores on the control group and they are not in the study."

I froze for a moment, then managed to stammer out that I had previously said I had no access to such data. He jumped up and slammed his hand down on his desk, breaking the pencil in half. He gave me a hard look.

"Goddammit, I told you I wanted that and I'm the one in charge and it will be done my way."

I stumbled out the door, ran to my car, and collapsed in tears. I could see my four years of hard work in the Ph.D. program evaporating. It had all been for nothing. I could not get that information and I would not get that desperately sought-after doctorate after all.

One of the first people I contacted was my statistics tutor, who had gone through a not-so-pleasant experience in obtaining his own Ph.D. He gave me the best advice I could ever have had. What research data could I obtain on regular university students regarding IQ and reading? After spending a week researching various studies pertaining to the reading performance of university students and any studies having to do with intelligence scores of university students, I hit upon an idea. There was a good amount of research on the reading rates of university students that I could cite in the study to compare with the LD group.

This fit perfectly with my study. I had measured the reading rate of every individual in the study. I compared the reading rate found in other studies of university students with the reading rates I obtained on my control group. They were all similar. When I compared the reading rate with the experimental group (students with learning disabilities), the rates were much lower, resulting in slower overall reading and taking longer to complete the test.

I discussed this with my tutor. His next piece of advice was to call the professor, and he provided very specific instructions about what to say.

I was nervous as I began speaking into the telephone. "Thank you for your suggestion," I began, "however, after researching the topic of IQs for university students, I found very little good research on this topic." I related the information I had collected about the flaws and outdated studies. He accepted my explanation about the lack of current research.

"I think I have found information that you will like, though, and find quite relevant to the study. I could compare the reading rates of the students in my study to those found in the research, and then compare those rates to the experimental group of students with learning disabilities."

Without hesitation the professor responded, "That's great. Do that and I'll sign off on the dissertation and I'm sure the other committee members will, too."

Oh my God. Relief flooded my body. I was so thankful for the advice I had received from my tutor. He knew the power that was often wielded by the "gatekeepers" and knew they could make or break you as a candidate. I didn't know what happened at other universities, but I suspected they were all similar. Maybe that was why so many people didn't ever finish their doctorate programs.

I knew the study I had fought so hard to have accepted would be of great value to students in higher education who had learning disabilities. The results proved (as my pilot study had proved) that students with learning disabilities read at a much slower rate than those without the disability. However, when given the extra time to complete the reading, their reading comprehension scores were basically the same as for the regular students.

The students with learning disabilities took an average of time-and-one-half to complete the twenty-minute test. The control group finished the reading test in the twenty minutes allowed, with the exception of a few students who had one or two comprehension questions to complete. The statistical analysis showed no significance between time and extra time scores for that group. The study proved that students with the extra time needed to complete the test performed as well as their non-learning disabled peers. This refuted the claim I had heard thousands of times from professors: "Anyone would do better with extra time."

This gave students with a nonvisible disability an equal chance to fulfill the dream of a college education.

Little did I realize that this study would prove to be very instrumental in changing attitudes and policies in higher education. Over the years the agencies providing entrance-level exams to professional schools gradually adopted policies to provide the accommodation to qualified students.

I was hired as a consultant by some of the agencies to assist in drafting policy. This led to being hired as a consultant to read documentation submitted by individuals requesting the accommodation. My job was to determine if the documentation submitted met the guidelines for identification of the disability, and if the individual met the guidelines of qualifying under the Americans with Disabilities Act (ADA). (It is now known as the Americans with Disabilities Act Amendments Act, or ADAAA).

Working toward my Ph.D. had been a long, arduous process. I had to keep telling myself that there was light at the end of the tunnel. I also made the decision not to put my personal life completely on hold. I didn't want to miss out on all the cultural activities that were available in San Francisco.

I was in a relationship with a man who was more than willing to expose me to one of his passions, the opera. I had never been to an opera. Some of the operas I attended were wonderful and I went more than once. During others, I confess I found it hard to stay awake. San Francisco was also a Mecca for the theater, which I loved. When I would become overwhelmed by my studies, I often took time to see a show.

Walking on the beach relieved some of my stress and the sights and sounds of the ocean helped to rejuvenate me and give me strength to keep pursuing that doctorate.

I made many new friends in San Francisco from all

walks of life. I loved my eclectic circle of companions. My yoga teacher was my age and had never learned how to drive, so her means of transportation were a bicycle and public transit. She had raised her children in the Haight Ashbury district during the 1960s, when that area was inhabited by hippies and famous performers such as Janis Joplin.

I had another lovely friend who volunteered to hold and caress crack-addicted babies at the University of California, San Francisco hospital. She always wore a string of pearls, even when in yoga classes, and she lived in the Upper Haight in a big Victorian house. She had been married to the man who wrote the hit song, "Mercedes Benz," for Janis Joplin. She told me a story once that left an impression on me. After her daughter smoked pot for the first time, she simply asked her, "How was it?" I thought that was so insightful as I never would have thought to do that, even if my kids had told me they were smoking pot. Back then I would have preached a sermon against such things. (I later found out that my kids *were* smoking pot.)

These friends added a new dimension to my life. After I obtained my doctorate, I became well acquainted with a different set of friends—some of the people who made up the social fabric of San Francisco. I had discovered that I needed to ascend the social ladder as well as the educational ladder if I wanted to be a success.

As I interacted with this group of people, I learned what they valued. Certainly education, cultural knowledge, and credentials, but also the proper conversation. Trying to fit in was nothing new for me. At age seventeen, I had studied the way the men in my office building held their utensils at lunch, and since that time I had worked hard to learn the "proper" way to do things. Anytime I was caught short, I made sure I didn't make the same mistake again.

Kay Graduating with Doctorate Degree

When I attended social functions, I was usually introduced as Dr. Runyan. The first question I was then asked was, "Where did you obtain your doctorate?" My answer, UC Berkeley, usually met the criteria of these individuals. My social life exposed me to much of what I considered to be superficial or trite. Most of the people I interacted with had been raised in fairly affluent families and they were also very well off, so I rarely elaborated on my upbringing and my long journey to obtain an education.

Even though I didn't speak of it, I never forgot my roots. I always identified with the underdog, the person who struggled and had to work much harder to achieve their goals, creating opportunities that many in my circle took for granted.

My relationship with the man who introduced me to the opera eventually ended. Once again, I had chosen a man who had different values and goals than I had. I didn't want to give up the hope that someday I would find success in my personal life, but in the meantime, I took comfort in my professional accomplishments.

14 A NEW PATH

I was ready to open my own private practice and retire from the university. I had worked at UC Berkeley for five years and was over fifty years old, so I met their requirements for retirement. I was concerned about not having a health insurance plan, but I believed that issue would be resolved soon by the Clinton Administration. Hilary Clinton was drafting a health care plan for all Americans; in my naïveté I thought the plan would be passed by the Senate and House, but it was not. Fortunately, I now had the earning capacity to be able to afford the outrageous premium I had to pay for health insurance as a private practitioner.

My dissertation results were now being read by many in higher education, and as a result, I was asked to be an expert witness in several cases involving students who were denied extra time on exams. This accommodation was then "trickled up" to law schools and all other professional schools. I was asked to present my research many times in the United States at major educational conferences. Then I started getting requests to present it in other countries, such as England, Austria, and New Zealand. I even went to China as part of a delegation from U.S. universities to present my findings to a group of university educators and dignitaries in Beijing.

My private practice in San Francisco was fully staffed and the business was gaining success. We offered tutoring services for preparing students for all tests, such as the GRE (entrance to graduate school exam), MCAT (entrance to medical school exam), LSAT (entrance to law school), et cetera, as well as the SAT for lower-grade students. I had trained my students in the specialized techniques that students with learning disabilities needed to compensate for their weak areas. These students were encouraged to ask for the extra time they were entitled to.

I continued providing psycho-educational test batteries for identification purposes. I met many adults who had struggled for years, not knowing they had learning disabilities, thinking they were just "dumb" because they were not good readers. They chastised themselves for not reading for pleasure, unaware of why the task was so arduous that it did not provide pleasure. I encouraged them to sign up for books on tape through an agency that provided all textbooks and literature on tape for the blind and dyslexic. Students could request that a particular book be put on tape, and it was a great way for students to get the information they needed.

My business continued to flourish. I added a private school in conjunction with the San Francisco School District. There were always children in special education classes whose educational needs were not being met and therefore were not succeeding. Parents were often looking for an alternative. My school could meet the needs of these students because we offered small classes with one-on-one help.

The school district paid for these students to attend my school. My teachers had to be fully credentialed, as I was. As time went on, though, I had great difficulty finding good special education teachers. After three years I closed the school portion of my business.

It had been a success, and I knew I had helped students who wouldn't have remained enrolled in school otherwise.

The consulting branch of my business continued to expand. I was contracted by various law schools and bar examiners to read documentation submitted by students who were requesting extra time. If ADHD was involved, they often requested a quieter environment for taking the exam. As the accommodations have evolved, the students obtaining the accommodation who are taking the bar exam are usually tested with other students receiving the same accommodation. Many times there are only six to ten students in the room.

I felt a great sense of pride in having contributed to the changes that have allowed students with learning disabilities and attention deficit disorder to achieve their goals for higher education. Research has shown that this group of people has traditionally been underemployed. Many have above-average intelligence and many are in the gifted range. However, due to the inability in many cases to pass timed exams in the workplace for a promotion, this group of individuals has not been able to climb the ladder to greater success.

As my private practice and consulting work continued to thrive, opera was not the only cultural experience I enjoyed. San Francisco had a huge culture centered around Argentine tango. I loved to dance, so I attended a few dances and was immediately hooked. I started taking lessons from the most experienced teachers in San Francisco and discovered dances were held in the city every night of the week. When the president of the Bay Area Tango Association moved to Mexico, I was nominated to fill the position. During my tenure as president, I brought many instructors from Buenos Aires to San Francisco.

One of My Tango Dance Partners

When I danced with the instructors, I was too nervous to experience the "three minutes of intimacy" that is part of the Argentine tango, where the man leads the woman so flawlessly that she forgets about her feet and gets lost in the music. I did not experience this with most of my American dance partners, probably because they were concentrating so heavily on learning the steps to this difficult dance that they could not focus on making their partners look as good as possible. I did eventually connect with two partners who were able to master this technique.

I decided I had to travel to Argentina and experience more. Accompanied by a friend, we flew to Buenos Aires for the "Congreso," taught by the best-of-the-best instructors. For one week I attended afternoon lessons, then danced from ten o'clock at night until two or three o'clock in the morning. This is when I truly learned what was meant by "three minutes of intimacy."

Three Minutes of Intimacy

Kay and Artist, Buenos Aires

Three minutes refers to the general length of the tango song. The woman must trust and surrender to her partner completely as he moves her around the floor with only slight pressure of his palm to the small of her waist. The sensuality, movement and pulsating rhythm of the music take over. There is no one there but the man and the woman and the music. His eyes are fiercely locked on hers, exuding strength and passion. Not a word is uttered, but they are passionately and totally connected. When the dance is over, the gentleman may say, "uno mas," meaning "one more dance."

The Argentine man never comes over to the table where a woman is sitting to ask for a dance. Rather than risk a public rejection, he catches her eye and gives a slight nod of his head. If she wants to dance with him, she gives a slight nod of her head in return, always keeping the eye contact. It is only then that he comes to her table and gallantly leads her to the floor for "three minutes of intimacy." Subtle gazing around the room continues throughout the evening, assuring that no one misses the opportunity to experience that "three minutes of intimacy."

I found myself trying to experience every part of the tango culture. In Argentina, people leave work at noon and go to the nearest public square in order to dance the tango for an hour. On any given day, dancers and boom boxes can be found most everywhere.

During my week in Argentina, I sought out a well-known artist and asked him to create posters for the next "Tango by the Bay Ball." Each time I visited his studio to check his progress, he turned on tango music and we danced. He presented me with a painting that represented the "three minutes of intimacy," and I have treasured that painting for many years. It occupies a special place in my home.

Even the trip to the airport to return home was fun. My friend and I checked out of our hotel but locked up our bags to be picked up later. Then the taxi cab driver we had come to know over the course of a week picked us up and rushed us to an afternoon tango so we could dance until the very last minute. We changed into our street clothes in the back seat of the taxi as we raced to the airport. Suddenly our driver pulled over to the side of the Autopista (freeway), jumped out, grabbed his CD player from the trunk of the car, inserted a tango CD, and started singing at the top of his lungs. When we arrived at the airport, we all hugged as if we were old friends.

Upon my return to San Francisco, it was time to start planning for the ball. I had been so inspired by my time in Argentina that I was determined to make it the best ball ever. I booked the beautiful City Hall building with its stunning marble floors and huge marble staircase. The dance area was large, and guests loved the catered dinner and professional photographer who was on hand to take individual pictures.

Although the ball was a great success, I knew my experience with the tango in America would never equal the enjoyment of that week I spent in Argentina. So after the "Tango by the Bay Ball," I never danced tango again.

I had always loved the theater, so my next foray was into acting. I enrolled in the Jean Shelton Acting Theater in San Francisco, which offered acting classes at night. I enjoyed acting, but I simply didn't have enough time to devote myself to the theater. Ms. Shelton suggested I get some "head shots" taken and try to land print or commercial work. I was excited when I was hired for a nonspeaking part in the "Nash Bridges" television series, which was filmed in San Francisco. I was cast as the mother of the groom in a wedding scene. The comedy duo of Cheech and Chong had a reoccurring role on the show, and they added excitement to the filming.

Kay and Kathie Lee Gifford

Filming took place on Treasure Island in a large tent. It was freezing cold, but of course no coats were allowed in a wedding scene. The young girls who played bridesmaids had it even worse than I did, as they were dressed in short, strapless dresses.

My agent secured other film roles for me. One of the most exciting jobs was when I was flown to New York by Kathie Lee Gifford to film an infomercial for her line of facial products. Not only was I put up in a great hotel, I was able to enjoy the nightlife of New York.

An additional perk was that I was finally able to meet—for the first time—two people with whom I had consulted for many months. One individual was from the Brooklyn Law School and another was from New York Law School. A few years later, the lady from Brooklyn Law School moved to San Francisco with her husband and I hired her for my private practice.

It was during this period of my life that I met and dated August Coppola, the father of actor Nicolas Cage and brother of director Francis Ford Coppola.

Kay and August Coppola, Savannah, Georgia

August was retired from San Francisco State University and had been a major contributor to the success of the film program at the university several years earlier. He regaled me with many stories and we had a lot of fun together. He later passed away in Newport Beach, California, and the *San Francisco Chronicle* devoted nearly a full page to his life.

These experiences enriched my life tremendously and provided me with many fond memories.

The twenty years I spent in San Francisco were in many ways the best years of my life.

15 MORE ADVENTURES

My life continued to evolve, and in 2004 I made the decision to relocate to Reno, Nevada.

The move was prompted by the fact that I had been appointed the legal guardian for a grandson who lived in Reno. Fortunately, I was at a point in my life where I could close my practice but keep working as a consultant and expert witness.

I soon realized, however, that I was going to need more income than my consulting provided. I had a preadolescent child to raise and I was his sole support.

I had already discovered that it wasn't easy to "break the ice" with people in Reno, particularly those in the field of education. What could I do that would provide the income I needed? I finally settled on a business that was unrelated to education.

Owning and operating elder care residential group homes.

For many years people from California and other states had chosen to retire in Nevada. The big bonus was no state income tax. As these retirees aged, it was becoming clear that Nevada did not have enough facilities for those who needed care. Small facilities in particular—regular houses in neighborhoods surrounded by families—were in short supply. Many of the homes that did exist were far from offering the best care, best meals, and caregivers who were reliable and willing to stay on the job. One of the reasons for the high turnover of caregivers was that most were underpaid, often making minimum wage or close to it. Many were paid under the table, with no opportunity to pay into Social Security or Unemployment Insurance.

I had purchased my mother's house in Oregon several years earlier as a rental investment. I decided to sell it and buy a new home for my venture. The area in which I had purchased my own home, South Reno, was booming with new construction. I found a suitable house in a new development just two miles away. Five bedrooms, exactly what I wanted. Six elderly, unrelated individuals (the maximum allowed due to residential zoning) would be able to live in the house.

I chose the name, "Magnolia House." I was probably influenced by my southern upbringing, as I envisioned a home that would offer genteel and gracious living.

Start-up was very expensive. A sprinkler system had to be installed in the ceiling and other modifications made. No residents could move in until I had the entire house furnished and I had hired caregivers.

I jumped through all the hoops of licensing, inspections, fingerprinting, and studying for two months to take the state administrator exam. I hired two Filipina ladies and agreed to sponsor them until they could obtain their green cards. This commitment was a little scary for me, as it meant that I had to keep them employed until they could apply for their green cards. I worried about the possibility that even if they didn't perform their job duties satisfactorily, I would still have to keep them employed. Fortunately, they were wonderful and kind to my residents and the families loved them. I placed them on my payroll so they could contribute to Social Security along with my required contribution as the employer.

After the first year, I gave them two days of paid vacation, figuring that with their regularly scheduled two days off, they would have four consecutive days of vacation. Eventually I paid them for a full week off.

They were also paid a good hourly wage. Most caregivers in Reno were Filipina and were not receiving the same pay and benefits. Consequently, these caregivers stayed with me for the twelve years I owned the elder care homes.

I eventually bought another home and it was licensed for five residents, so I ended up with eleven beds. This venture gave me the money I needed to meet the expenses of a grandchild's needs and enough money for his college education.

I truly enjoyed my elderly residents. One of the first ladies to move in was in good physical condition but was developing dementia. Penny was very chatty and carried her purse on her arm wherever she went in the house, even to the table for meals. One Halloween we dressed her in a costume and told her that her job was to hand out candy to the trick-or-treaters. She was thrilled. The doorbell rang, and she opened the door to find about six children under eight years of age standing there. I held the bowl of candy and told her to put some in each child's bag. She took a handful of candy and crammed it into her purse.

"No, Penny," I said. "Give it to the children."

She continued stuffing candy into her purse.

"I'm not giving those little shits my candy!" she said.

The mothers were horrified by this comment, as was I. I quickly deposited candy into each child's bag as one of the caregivers convinced Penny to go into another room.

We laughed about that incident for a week and decided we should ask someone else to hand out the candy next Halloween.

Penny shared the large master bedroom suite with

another resident and they became great pals. However, as Penny's dementia worsened, she started getting up at night and putting her roommate Janet's house slippers under her own pillow. One night the caregiver on duty heard a startling comment through the monitor that was installed in their room.

"Penny! Give me my goddamn slippers and get your scrawny butt back in bed!"

This was from a sweet lady who never said a bad word, so of course we were all shocked.

Janet had been a docent at the old opera house in Virginia City, Nevada, for many years. Sometimes she thought she was still on the job. Each time I came to the house, she greeted me with, "Hello, Dear Heart, how are you today?" If I brought prospective families over to tour the house, Janet gave me my usual greeting before asking, "May I give these lovely people the tour of the house?"

She was a wonderful tour guide, letting them know about the food and the activities that were offered every day. Janet was 95 years old and often regaled us with stories of her childhood, spent in the authentic "Wild West." Virginia City, Nevada, was very remote at that time and many of the inhabitants were cowboys, Native Americans, and sometimes unsavory people who were in trouble with the law. Many of Janet's stories revolved around the Native American children who visited her house frequently.

At my own house I tended three big raised garden beds where every summer, I grew green beans, squash, green peas, radishes, and a multitude of other vegetables that I thought the residents might like. The ladies loved to sit at the table and snap green beans for dinner. I showed them how to blanch the green beans after snapping them in boiling water for a minute, then plunging them into ice water to cool before they were bagged and frozen for future meals.

There was no sitting and vegging out in front of the television. I hired a fitness trainer three times a week so the ladies could participate in chair exercises. Two to three times a week, the caregivers would play bingo with those who wanted to play.

We rarely had a man as a resident but when we did, we found that he usually reacted differently to losing his independence than the ladies did. One man in particular was very difficult. I knew I was in for trouble when his paperwork was completed and his son stood up, shook my hand, and said, "He's all yours now." He said goodbye to his father and hurried out the door to catch his plane back to Texas.

His dad had been a career military guy and liked to give orders, not take them. He refused to eat with the ladies, refused to let the caregivers change his Depends, and defied every suggestion made to him. After the ladies finished their meals, the caregivers warmed up his meals in the microwave oven and served him at the table—alone. Since he saw his food being warmed up in the microwave oven, he became convinced it was not a home-cooked meal. As soon as the plate was set in front of him, he swiped it off the table onto the floor.

No amount of bribery could change his behavior. His bedding and clothing had to be laundered two to three times a day and plastic had to be placed on any chair he used.

After many unsuccessful attempts to get him to comply, I asked to have a chat with him in his room. I explained that since his level of care had become more complex and required more of the caregivers' time, I was raising his monthly rate by five hundred dollars. That got his attention and he stopped his bad behaviors. He still had some incontinence accidents between changes, but he began eating with the other residents and eventually turned into a really nice old man. During the three years he lived in Magnolia House, his children did not visit once.

Other families did, though, and they appreciated being able to drop in at any time, without notice. All the families chose to have their loved one pass away at the Magnolia House with hospice care to keep them comfortable.

I must admit I had a very hard time with the passing of my residents. Hospice put them on Code Pink when their time came, which was usually thought to be in two or three days. I started saying goodbye to each one just before the Code Pink designation. I could no longer sit and watch them die, but saying goodbye was very important to me. The caregivers and their family members were there with them until the end.

In the meantime, my grandson and I had many ups and downs, but we both persevered and came out of that time period for the better. He went off to college and I had a lot of time to consider my future.

I didn't care for Reno at all. The high desert, dust, and altitude had never been to my liking. Twelve years in the elder care business was enough, even though I loved the experience and the richness of knowledge the elderly residents had to offer. I decided it was time for me to move on again. I was able to sell my two elder care homes quickly, since they were full and I had a wait list.

I was nearing the end of my time in Reno, and my birthday was approaching. I decided to throw a big party for myself before leaving town. To accommodate the schedule of one of my girlfriends, I eventually decided to throw two parties—one for the men and one for the women.

I had a number of platonic male friends and I had continued to date during the years I lived in Reno. Since I was still friends with all my former boyfriends, I invited them, too. The invitation read: *Birthday Party for Kay – Bar-b-cue, Karaoke Singing, and Guaranteed Fun. No Presents Please.*

I hadn't told any of my ex-boyfriends who else would be

in attendance, and I immediately began worrying that they would think I was crazy. I was surprised when all twelve of the men I invited showed up.

As I announced that I was honoring my friends and former boyfriends, they all looked around the room. I knew they were probably trying to figure out who the "boyfriends" were. We turned on the karaoke machine after dinner and my ex-boyfriend Lou volunteered to sing. I had met him at "Karaoke Night" at the Nugget Casino.

Everyone got into the spirit of the evening and cheered on the guests who had the courage (after a few cocktails) to try to sing karaoke, no matter how good or bad they were. They had all brought me presents even though they were instructed not to, and they seemed to know exactly what kind of gifts I would like. Afterwards, I received many texts telling me that it was the best party they had ever attended.

I wanted to leave Reno in a blaze of glory and I did!

At seventy-four years of age, I moved back to Eugene, Oregon, the place I left at age sixteen when I married my children's father, Tom. Free to move anywhere I wanted, I had considered returning to San Francisco, but realized that the city had become far too expensive, so I opted to return to Oregon. I had a history in Eugene, a kinship with the town even after a fifty-seven-year absence. And my parents were buried there.

In the beginning I didn't know a soul, so I had a lot of time to walk the streets surrounding my house and wonder why I hadn't "found myself" earlier in life—or if I ever would.

I resolved to finish writing my life story, which I had begun years earlier while living in Reno. Perhaps the process of writing about my life would lead me to find myself.

My life had been marked by traumatic events as well as my own poor choices, made as a result of circumstances and ignorance. Unable to experience life outside of the walls of poverty in which I lived for so long, I had no idea I could have chosen a different way of living at an earlier age.

God gave me the strength to rise above adversity, even the consequences of some of my own decisions. I eventually learned from my mistakes and was able to make something of myself, helping others in the process.

In spite of her sometimes harsh parenting, I learned most of what has guided me through life from my mother. Hope, faith, and creating opportunities where they don't exist were all values she taught me. Her faith in God kept her going against all odds. She was a survivor. I'm grateful to both my parents for instilling in their children the value of education.

My older brother Gerald, who was my "rock," and my older sister Barbara shared many of the struggles I did, although they did manage to make it to adulthood before Daddy had his "nervous breakdown." Gerald worked hard all his life. After working in sawmills and a stint in the Army, he went on to become a fireman and a well-respected arson inspector in Oregon. Barbara earned her Bachelor of Arts degree from Long Beach State during the time she was married and raising three young children. Ben joined the Air Force after high school, attended flight school after being discharged, and worked as a pilot for Delta Airlines for the next forty years.

As of this writing Gerald and Barbara are in very poor health and I am aware I don't have much time left with them. Ben passed away eight years ago, along with his son, doing what he loved to do—flying one of the vintage planes from the collection he had acquired over the years.

As for my children, my oldest son works in the field of information technology, my daughter is a business owner, and my youngest son is employed in the biological sciences at a local college. They have always been supportive of my endeavors and I'm proud of their accomplishments.

Kay-Doll, Kathy, Kay, Kathryn... I have had many identities during my lifetime but now I am simply "Kay," a woman who has overcome a lot and accomplished some things I never imagined. Like everyone else, I have regrets. For some reason, I think about the things I didn't do right more than those I did do right.

Now that I am back in Eugene, I have visited my parents' grave, placing flowers at the head of the double stone bearing their names. I reflect on my lack of a relationship with my father. I regret that as an adult, I could have tried to foster a relationship but I had accepted the fact that Daddy didn't converse with me. I didn't know how to change that. During our infrequent visits, I remember how I wanted Daddy to acknowledge that I had made something of myself, but he never did.

I, however, knew that I had made my life a success.

ACKNOWLEDGMENTS

I would like to thank all the individuals who were instrumental in helping me write this book.

The High Sierra Writers Group sponsored many wonderful presentations about the craft of writing. My fellow critique group members, including Gina Noel Decker, Lucy Dupertuis, Patricia Graap, Geri Young, and Carol Taylor, provided helpful comments and suggestions. I also received insightful feedback from a number of beta readers, including Barbara Hancock, Joyce Nash, Maria Palace, and Valene Georges.

In addition, many friends read portions of my book and encouraged me to continue writing.

The invaluable guidance of my editor, Stephanie McMullen, was much appreciated.

ABOUT THE AUTHOR

M. Kay Runyan, Ph.D., has dedicated her long career to working with individuals with dyslexia and attention deficit disorder. Her work has been published in scholarly journals and textbooks. She has contributed to the field through her research on accommodations for this group as required under the Americans With Disabilities Act.

Dr. Runyan is retired and lives in Eugene, Oregon. She enjoys spending time with her family, including four grandchildren and two great-grandchildren.

Made in the USA
Middletown, DE
06 July 2021